A CHURCH THE MOOR

CHRIST CHURCH, BIDDULPH MOOR

Bill Ridgway

Front cover: From watercolour painting by FH Watts 1936
Back cover: BM Petalers gather around their floral commemoration of the church's 150th anniversary.
L to R standing: Sandra Tomlinson, Carol Handley, (Chair BM Community Association) Mary Harley,
Silvia Bickley, Ann Moreton, Chris Holdsworth, Paula Whitelaw.
Foreground: James Capper, Liz Barrett, Emma Holdsworth, Sandra Beard, Leslie Murray.
Courtesy Biddulph Chronicle

CHURNET VALLEY BOOKS

6 Stanley Street, Leek, Staffordshire ST13 5HG 01538 399033

© Bill Ridgway & Churnet Valley Books 2014 ISBN 9781904546948
Any use of this book in any form needs the permission of the publisher.
All other rights reserved.

TO THE PEOPLE OF THE MOOR

Acknowledgements

I would like to thank the former vicar of Christ Church, Revd Andrew Dawswell, and the present incumbent, Revd Darren Fraser, for allowing me to use the church archive, and the staff at Biddulph Library for their help in providing additional reference material for this book. Thanks are also due to Paul Baker, former Property Manager of Biddulph Grange, for allowing me access to Edward Cooke's diaries. I'd like to express my gratitude to staff at the Stafford Records Office who were generous with their time and expertise, and to all the people who have donated photographs for this publication I would like to give a special thank you to Mr Terry Williams whose advice on all things technical proved invaluable.

To anyone else I may have forgotten, please accept my apologies and thanks.

Come Unto Me and I Will Give You Rest

Bill Ridgway

Bill Ridgway began his writing career in education, producing a wide range of books for the schools' market. On his retirement from teaching, he turned to local history writing. His books, *Potteries Lad, Biddulph Moor Within Living Memory, Knypersley Recalled, More Potteries Lad* and *Bateman's World* are published by Churnet Valley Books. Bill is married with two children, and lives in the Staffordshire Moorlands.

CONTENTS

Author's note
Introduction

Author's Note

Writing local history is like doing a jigsaw puzzle, but with pieces missing and no picture on the lid. You assemble the bits you have and, hopefully arrive at the right conclusions.

In the case of Christ Church archive, I've been relatively lucky. Most of the puzzle is there, albeit scattered in various files, because the church's first incumbent, the Revd Francis Gordon, threw very little away. His successors were also disinterested enough to leave his accumulation of papers, forms, bills, invoices, receipts and letters in their folders awaiting an obsessive optimist who'd try and make sense of it all.

The experience has not been without its rewards. Trawling through the bric-a-brac of the church's first ten years has brought me face to face with the major players of the time and hinted at their character. It's also shed light on the hierarchical nature of Victorian society, where a few wealthy landowners were vastly outnumbered by unschooled workers whose name was often reduced to a cross on paper.

If James Bateman of Biddulph Grange was fund-raiser and delegator and Francis Gordon his right-hand man, Joseph Stanway was the stonemason and master builder who, with teams of local workmen, brought the project to fruition. And the people of the moor, who gave of their mites and their time, were the beneficiaries of the Sunday Service and the Book of Common Prayer. It was in the National School, opposite the church gates, that their children would learn to read and write and in a few years render a mark on paper redundant.

What follows is the story of the foundation of Christ Church and its first congregations. It's a story located in a particular time and place, but universal for all that.

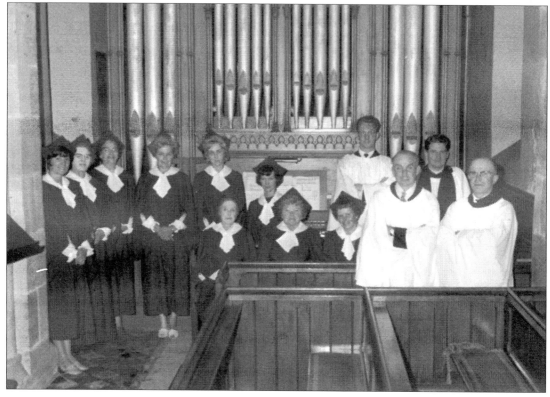

The church choir in the mid 60s.
L to R standing at back: Mabel Yeomans nee Alcock, Hannah Shufflebotham, Ellen Lancaster, Freda
Biddulph, Elizabeth Tweet née Mitchell, Miriam Leese, Robert Yeomans, Revd Ian Stephenson.
L to R below: Nelly Beech, Mrs Iken, Cynthia Brassington, Percy Mitchell, Mr Simcock.

Revd McGuire's painting party, mid 1980s.
A section of the church was painted the day after Boxing Day each year on a two-year rota.

INTRODUCTION

An unseasonal snow fell on Biddulph Moor in the last week of October, 1859. James Bateman's wife, Maria retired to her room as the outside temperature plummeted and the lake at Biddulph Grange froze over.

Bateman's friend, the artist Edward Cooke, who Bateman had brought from Congleton Station a few days earlier, had to content himself making designs for the 'Egypt' section of the gardens and sketching out possible lay-outs for the 'model' village proposed for Biddulph Moor. By mid-week, south-westerly gales had bought heavy rain, turning the roads to slush and confining Bateman, his son John and Cooke to the Billiards Room for the evening.

Rain and high winds persisted throughout the following day, but did little to disperse the snow which continued to blanket the gardens. Again, Cooke opened his sketch book. and settled to make his first, tentative sketches of what he called 'the Lombard church for the moor'.

On the 27th October, the weather had improved sufficiently for Mr Weston, the curate on the moor, to pay an early visit with his wife to the Grange. For the past three years he'd been holding Sunday services in the National School which faced the site where the new church was to be built. After a late breakfast, Cooke showed Weston the sketches he'd made of the proposed church.

Bateman was the main mover behind the building of Christ Church.

Cooke and Bateman had a taste for the Lombard, or Italianate, style of architecture.

This ambitious Italianate building was originally envisaged by Bateman and Cooke.

The Grange, much of it designed by Bateman's own hand, owed its principal features - the arched windows, belvedere, and low roofs - to the style, and both men had enjoyed vacations in Italy, where grand Italianate buildings overlooked the square in almost every town. The idea was that the church on the moor would echo their preference, and the Westons were equally enthusiastic.

Their plans met with further encouragement on Cooke's next visit to the Grange in June the following year. Before visiting a range of orchid houses which had recently been built by Bateman at Knypersley Hall, Archdeacon Rushton of Blackburn and the Revd Francis Gordon were invited to give their stamp of approval. Other clergymen, including Bateman's uncle William Holt, were asked to contribute their suggestions regarding the roughed out design.

A study of the preliminary sketches prompted some reservations, and adjustments were made. A year would pass before , on 7th June, 1861, a more detailed plan was produced by Cooke and passed over to Bateman, whose contributions were necessary if the project was to be successful. Unfortunately, the question of cost now constrained Cooke's original vision, and a radical re-appraisal produced a church more Norman in style, but which retained the arched windows and rounded apse common to both Norman and Italianate design. His ambition for a grand Lombard bell tower was also tempered by economic reality.

Cooke was occupied with other schemes when he paid his next visit to Biddulph in the September of 1861 - one of which was the exhumation of the 'cromlech' in what was then Bateman's deer park behind the Warder's Tower at Knypersley Lake. Among those joining Bateman and Cooke was Professor Richard Owen, the director of London's Natural History Museum and the man responsible for coining the word 'dinosaur'.

Bateman's house, Biddulph Grange.
The Church Building Committee met here for the first time in June 1860.

Two years later Cooke wrote in his diary: 'Went to see Bob's studio. [Bateman's son, Robert's studio in Biddulph Old Hall.] All went up to Knypersley [Hall] and took luncheon in the new garden house. Drove to the moor and saw the church and parsonage.'

The date of his entry is August 13th, 1863. By then the church on the moor was a named reality - Christ Church - and its first incumbent, Francis Gordon, had been welcoming the congregation through its doors since its consecration on May 28th that year.

1. STATE OF THE NATION

Christ Church was built at a time when Britain's industrial might was unchallenged. Its empire was growing, discoveries and developments in all fields were constantly being made, new railways linked towns which a generation before had been served by coach and cart and the scientific disciplines we now take for granted were fast becoming established.

But the country which kicked off the industrial revolution also inherited its problems. The influx of work-seeking villagers into the expanding towns and cities led to overcrowding, crime, poor sanitation and a steep rise in infant mortality. Solutions were offered from many quarters; it was in the interests of industrialists to maintain a constant supply of healthy labour; it was the church's job to alleviate poverty where they found it, and concerned individuals with wealth and a social conscience were more able to bend the government's ear to the plight of the poor than their less well-placed peers leaving the factory gates.

Bateman was fortunate to have benefited from the surge of wealth then being created by the can-do Victorians. While taking his privilege for granted, he was also aware of the ignorance and spiritual poverty on his doorstep, and saw it as his duty to address these twin evils. His mission was to save souls on the moor, and to give their owners a church worthy of the task.

Turbulent years at home

Bateman was in his late twenties when Victoria came to the throne, and much water had flowed under the bridge between then and the building of Christ Church. Britain had become the world's powerhouse, and a new history was being forged by the day. In 1852, when Biddulph Moor National School took in scholars for the first time, the postal service introduced pillar boxes on Jersey, the Free Library opened its doors in Manchester, the first undersea telegraph was laid between Anglesey and Ireland and the Great Ormond Street Hospital for sick children took in its first patients.

In the same year, Queen Victoria opened the Houses of Parliament (rebuilt after the fire of 1834), Isambard Kingdom Brunel and Digby Wyatt prepared their designs for a more grandiose Paddington Station, Dickens published his novel *Bleak House* and the Duke of Wellington's funeral cortege was mourned by thousands lining the route to St Paul's. By the end of the year, Burma had become the latest British colony.

This tidal-wave of national events was no less impressive in the year the church was built. The world's first underground railway (the Metropolitan Line) carried thousands of passengers under the London streets for the first time that year; Yorkshire County Cricket Club was founded in Sheffield, the newly-formed football association laid down the rules of the game in a Holborn pub, Broadmoor Asylum opened its doors to the criminally insane and clergyman Charles Kingsley's novel *The Waterbabies* - a morality tale still popular today - was snapped up in the bookshops. Closer to home, a young couple holidaying in Rudyard decided to name their first born son after the lake. Rudyard Kipling was born two years later.

But for all that it was a turbulent era at home and abroad. Cooke's diary for February, 1848, noted the uprising in France, which toppled the French king. Two months later, he wrote: 'The Chartist meeting went off quietly'. The Chartists were regarded as a serious threat to the status quo by the upper classes - including Cooke and Bateman - and as encouraging the unrest which had brought revolution to the rest of Europe, helped along the way by Karl Marx's *Communist Manifesto*.

Yet the People's Charter was hardly life-threatening. Its aims - to give every man over 21 a vote, to adopt a secret ballot, and to pay MPs so that a man no longer had to be wealthy to enter parliament - were all adopted not long after the movement came to an end. After a ten year struggle the Chartists lost their battle. Their final rally, called in 1848 at Kennington Common, London, now attracted few supporters due to heavy rain and the presence of armed troops.

Chartism was not the only sign of discontent simmering beneath the surface of working-class life. Pit explosions were commonplace, and the low wages paid to mill workers was scant reward for long hours worked and the arduous labour involved. Until 1853, transportation to Australia commonly awaited those accused of instigating strikes, and workers involved in forming an 'association' faced summary dismissal. It was not until 1844, less than twenty years before the building of Christ Church, that the new Mines Act prohibited women and children under ten from underground work in the collieries.

Farm labourers fared little better in the countryside where they earned such meagre wages they were driven to riot. Women, too, had their grievances, notably in Wales in 1843, where the Carmarthen workhouse was destroyed in an attention-grabbing plea for 'better food and liberty'. Others, like Elizabeth Fry, Mary Somerville and Florence Nightingale relied on grit and determination to achieve reforms and to secure the same privileges in the emerging professions as men.

Discontent at work was exacerbated by conditions in the home. The population had risen by 25% between 1840 and 1860, and the congregation at the 'church on the moor' would be drawn from an unprecedented twenty-two million now living in Britain. The struggle to accommodate this huge increase gave rise to slums where twelve in a house was commonplace, cholera endemic and basic food frequently in short supply.

Advances in hygiene and medicine, however, did occur. Epidemics of smallpox were greatly reduced from 1853, when vaccination for infants was made compulsory. A year later, Dr John Snow prevented an outbreak of cholera in London by removing the handle of a public pump, thus proving that contaminated water, and not polluted air, was responsible for its transmission. Even so, it would be 1875 before Bazalgette built an adequate sewage system under the capital, thus following in the footsteps of the Romans, who'd dug the Cloaca Maxima under Rome a few thousand years before.

Conditions among the poor in England might have been bad, but in Ireland and the Scottish Highlands they were dire. Ireland, always simmering over the question of independence, was now brought to the brink of starvation. From 1846 to 1849 blight devastated the potato crop, leaving those who were able with no alternative but to emigrate - many to America.

Revd Edwin Wheeldon (1905-1920) seated centre front alongside Christ Church choirboys.
Wheeldon went on to become Vicar of St Michael's, Horton.

Sixty years on, Revd John McGuire (!971-2000) 4th from the left, joins Christ Church choristers for the camera.

The church

The turbulent years of mid-Victorian Britain affected all aspects of society, not least the church, which was fighting battles of its own. Bateman and Cooke, both staunchly Church of England, were starkly aware of the competition for souls. By the 1850s, it not only had to fight its corner against non-conformist rivals, such as Methodists, Congregationalists, Quakers and Unitarians, but an increasingly vociferous clamour among some of its own clergy who declared that the Church of England should seek spiritual truth in the rituals and devotions of the Roman Catholic church.

To add to its woes, the church found its fundamental beliefs challenged by the latest scientific discoveries. Darwin's *On the Origin of Species*, published in 1859, was a huge blow to those whose life had been defined by their faith. Evolution, not God, was the new buzz-word, and it was all but impossible for some to reconcile themselves to its implications.

Bateman was not put off. He built his Geological Gallery at the Grange in defiance of Darwin's claims. And during that snowy October of 1859, he and Cooke were at work preparing a further response to the upheaval - the church on the moor.

Trouble abroad

Few empires are forged without putting about a bit of stick. The British Empire, though tolerant compared to others, was not averse to sending in the heavy mob when the situation demanded it, and in the mid 19th century was variously involved in wars and skirmishes in Africa, Afghanistan, China, India, Russia and New Zealand. (Despite a loss in trade, it managed to steer clear of the American Civil War of 1861.)

Some colonial apologists found it difficult to understand why native peoples didn't necessarily agree that the take-over of their country by a foreign power was a good idea. After all, the British were there as much to civilise as to avail themselves of its natural resources - and they *did* bring railways and order.

Such musings found little sympathy among some of the co-opted Indian troops, whose hostility to British rule led to widespread revolt in 1857 and the massacre of British officers and their families. It took over a year of bloody reprisals to stamp out the uprising, by which time many garrisons held out only by dint of good fortune.

Four years earlier, the British had again been at war, this time with Russia in the Crimea. The Russians had been bent on taking over the Ottoman Empire, ostensibly to protect orthodox Christians living there. An enlarged Russia was not in Britain's interests, and a fleet was sent to join the allied French squadron near the Dardanelles. Russia ignored the warning, and war was declared on 26th March 1854. Commander-in-Chief Lord Raglan, who'd lost an arm at Waterloo, was ordered to prevent the Russians seizing Istanbul and to attack their positions at Sevastopol.

The first battle of the war was won by the British and French, who secured high land above the River Alma and drove the Russians off the field. A month later, the British suffered heavy losses when a misunderstood order to attack well-defended Russian positions was given. Only 426 returned out of the 673 who'd taken part in this 'Charge of the Light Brigade', as Tennyson called it in his famous poem.

By 1855, the British and French had secured the key town of Sevastopol - aided by the Russians blowing up their own magazines before fleeing - and a year later, in March 1856, the Treaty of Paris was signed. The Crimean War had been won, but at a price. As many soldiers succumbed to cholera, dysentery and typhus as had died in battle. Had it not been for the indefatigable Florence Nightingale and her team of nurses working round the clock at Scutari hospital, the death-toll would have been much higher. Kick-starting a revolution in hygiene, she introduced modern nursing to the world and reduced the death-rate at Scutari from 42 per 100 to 22 per 1000.

The Crimean victory was greeted in Britain with wild rejoicing. Edward Cooke was creating a stumpery in his London gardens (the stumps sent by James Bateman, one weighing half a ton) when the news came through. He wrote in his diary: 'At ten at night they fired 101 guns for news of peace, just arrived'.

The scholars at Biddulph Moor National School, opened four years earlier, would have been equally jubilant.

Exciting times

Victory at war wasn't the only feather in the British cap. Though it may not have seemed so to those sending their malnourished sons to the local ragged school for a few hours a week, mid-century Britain was by far the richest country in the world. Its inventive genius, military conquests and financial acumen secured it abundant raw materials and opened international markets for its products. It would take Europe, mired in revolution and internal friction, a generation to catch up. And there was much catching up to do. A list of British achievements at this time is sufficiently impressive to legitimate the claim that today's world began here. And it began with steam.

In 1860, when Bateman and Cooke rode the footplate of the first locomotive to trundle down the Biddulph Valley Line, they were trading on a railway history going back to 1829, when George Stephenson came up with the idea of increasing locomotive efficiency by driving heat through a multi-tube boiler, rather than a single pipe as had been the case with the first primitive pit-engines. The Rocket was an instant success, and within fifteen years railway mania had taken over.

By 1838, the first train had been cheered into Birmingham from London, and with five hundred miles of track already laid, could have gone on to Liverpool. Euston Station's eye-arresting Doric arch, completed in the same year, ousted any doubt that the age of the train had arrived.

Three years later, the Anglo-French genius Isambard Kingdom Brunel completed his 118 mile wide-gauge line from a newly-opened Paddington terminus to Bristol, carving a two mile tunnel through Box Hill in the process. Brunel epitomised Victorian confidence, anything was possible and innovations in engineering were created daily. If steam was good enough for trains, it was good enough for ocean-going vessels. His steam-ship, *Great Western*, launched in 1837, was enthusiastically greeted by the crowds in New York on its successful maiden voyage to America the following year.

His next ship, *Great Britain*, launched by Prince Albert in 1843, was even more ambitious. This 328 foot leviathan was the first ocean-going screw-driven all-metal vessel and a new wonder even to those who'd witnessed another Brunel triumph three months earlier - the first tunnel under a navigable river (the Thames). The year's end was also marked by another memorable event, when Dicken's latest novel, *A Christmas Carol*, sold 6000 copies, thus entering the bestseller list within weeks of its publication. It would be 1864, a year after Christ Church was built, that Brunel's crowning glory, the Clifton Suspension Bridge, was completed.

Brunel was just one of an inexhaustible list of pioneers who assured Britain's place on the world stage. Bessemer, who patented his revolutionary steel-making process in 1855; Prince Albert, the driving-force behind the Great Exhibition of 1851 and Joseph Paxton, whose revolutionary Crystal Palace housed it; Macadam, whose roads knocked hours off journeys times; Fox Talbot, who made the photograph, rather than the sketch book, possible for the first time; Thomas Cook, who introduced the rail trip and package tour and brought both within the pocket of the man in the street; George Cayley, whose coachman delivered the first manned flight in Cayley's glider (and afterwards gave notice); David

The Great Exhibition of 1851 marked Britain's role as the world's greatest industrial power.

Livingstone, the first white man to explore Africa's dark interior and who named the Victoria Falls after the British monarch; and Michael Faraday, who demonstrated for the first time how to generate electricity.

Despite the poverty of many and the inordinate wealth of the few, a new middle class was emerging. At home and abroad, the Union flag was fluttering and increasing patches of red were appearing on the world map. The country which gave the world Pimms No 1, the golf Open Championship, Cox's Pippin and the Grand National also gave it the Penny Black and the transatlantic cable. Along the way it introduced botany and horticulture to fern and orchid fanatics like James Bateman, whose quirkish Victorian gardens kept step with the upsurge of achievements elsewhere.

A church for the moor

This was the world familiar to James Bateman, Edward Cooke and the inhabitants of the moor. Christ Church and the National School were part of that world, and Bateman their mover and shaker. It can be claimed with some justification that these two buildings represented the birth of Biddulph Moor, which by 1863, instead of a scattered community of small farms and isolated cottages, became a village in its own right with a strong identity, and 'the church on the moor' at its centre.

The scene is reminiscent of the early industrialisation of the Biddulph Valley shortly before BM National School was built.

The Sunday School group in the Church Hall yard with their teachers around 1960.
The old Council School (1908), now Moor First, in background.

Revd Geraint James (1958-65) seated with young members of the
congregation/Sunday School while mothers look on.

2. BIRTH OF A VILLAGE

On Sunday, 14th September, 1854, the Bishop of Lichfield joined Cooke at the Batemans for lunch. Afterwards the party attended the service at St Lawrence's Church, where the Bishop offered prayers for the continued success of Biddulph Moor National School and the Red Cross School at Knypersley.

Bateman invited the congregation to tea at the Grange. After they'd eaten, they were free to admire the work being done on the gardens. The following day, while Cooke was busy instructing the estate workers on the 'fixing of stones about the grounds', Bateman drove the Bishop up to the moor to see the small temporary parsonage he'd built for the curates working on the moor under the direction of William Holt, and who were making use of a licence granting permission for Sunday services to be held in the National School until such a time as the church could be built.

Two years earlier, Bateman's coachman had driven Cooke and Maria Bateman up to the moor in the family brougham, where they met her husband to decide where this parsonage would be sited. After a brief exchange of ideas, a site on the Hurst was agreed, and they set off back. Cooke and Bateman went to work on its design the same evening, but Cooke, who was prone to boils, eye-strain and other physical ailments, retired early to his bed with a sore chest and a mustard plaster. He passed an uncomfortable night, but had sufficiently recovered later that week to make another journey to the moor.

The Tunstall turnpike

The school and the small Moor Parsonage were notable additions to the scattering of cottages and small farmsteads nearby. It would be another nine years before Christ Church became the prominent feature - in addition to the row of New Street cottages first sketched out by Edward Cooke in 1859.

Like many upland settlements, Biddulph Moor was an isolated community. The main Tunstall to Congleton turnpike was more than a mile away, narrow, and under constant repair due to the increase in trade between the emerging Potteries and nearby towns such as Congleton and Macclesfield. Uneven surfaces and heavier carts created havoc, particularly in winter, taking a toll on the animals and sometimes necessitating an additional (and expensive) horse to haul the loads.

Biddulph Valley was sparsely populated, with occasional dwellings dotted close by the road and few substantial buildings to the north apart from St Lawrence's Church and the as yet incomplete Biddulph Grange, which at the time lay adjacent to the road. To the south lay Bradley Green - now Biddulph - but this, too, was little more that a sprinkling of modest properties. It would only become a small town twenty years later, when Robert Heath arrived, introduced Black Bull colliery, and set about providing his miners and ironworkers with housing.

Unobstructed from view, the Batemans' private chapel at Red Cross - later St John's - and the school opposite were set in the midst of an endless tapestry of fields, here and there marked with the spoil heaps and headgear of small, privately owned

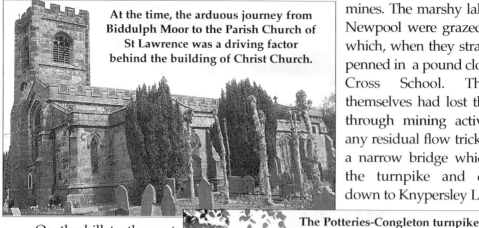

At the time, the arduous journey from Biddulph Moor to the Parish Church of St Lawrence was a driving factor behind the building of Christ Church.

The Potteries-Congleton turnpike was over a mile from Biddulph Moor.

mines. The marshy lake beds of Newpool were grazed by cows which, when they strayed, were penned in a pound close by Red Cross School. The lakes themselves had lost their water through mining activities and any residual flow trickled under a narrow bridge which carried the turnpike and continued down to Knypersley Lakes.

On the hill to the east stood Knypersley Hall, the residence of John Bateman and his wife Elizabeth. A high stone wall separated its grounds from the road, as is still the case. The mansion enjoyed uninterrupted views across the valley; the spire of their chapel was a prominent landmark from as far away as Mow Cop and would have struck the eye immediately on leaving Knypersley Hall for the Sunday Service. If the weather was inclement, the Batemans would drive their carriage down an estate avenue which emerged opposite a small colliery on Gutter Lane - now Park Lane - close to the site of Bateman Junior High School.

The rumble of coal carts was more frequent as the turnpike crested the rise to Childerplay. Here, mining activity was increasing rapidly to meet the insatiable demand for coal. Some of the mines were sufficiently profitable to invest in steam-powered winches and deeper shafts were dug to the richer seams. Others were little more than bell pits, worked by local farmers and their families to supplement their income.

For the moment, everything was hauled by cart or tramway. In 1859, when the railway arrived, that would all change. The clank of steam engines, the upsurge of deep-mine activity and the beat of forge-hammers which accompanied Robert Heath's arrival supplanted the tinkle of horse brass and the creak of the 3mph cart. But until then, the horse, trundling along the stone-chipped turnpike amid the silence of a pastoral landscape, was king.

An isolated community

Then, as now, two roads led from the turnpike to Biddulph Moor: Gutter Lane and Outwood Road - now Woodhouse Lane - which then took its name from Outwood Gate Farm near the summit. The roads were little more than tracks, maintained by the

Parish Board, whose surveyor had the responsibility of patching the craters scoured by rain and the passage of carts. Gutter Lane looked across a vale of fields to the north, some hedge-lined, others earth-banked, interspersed with copses and trees which overshadowed uncultivated rills. To the south, walls enclosed the Knypersley Hall estate, with lodge-guarded gates along the way. The lane was barely wide enough for two carts to pass.

Bateman had built his carriage drive from Biddulph Grange to Judgefield Lane during the 1850s, with a lodge at the intersection. Tracks to sporadic farm buildings led off as the road climbed; the mark of the quarryman was evident amid the outcrops of gritstone at its summit, from which St John's had been cut six years earlier.

The lane which continued to Biddulph Moor was equally narrow. The broken stone surface was pitted through exposure to wind, rain and winter blockages, when local families would join to rid the lane of snow. Outwood Road had the additional encumbrance of a sharp and twisting descent into Biddulph Valley, culminating in what is now Smithy Lane. An ancient packhorse track also cut up from what became Broadmeadows. It passed the 17th century Nettlebeds Farm, following the contours of the hill and striking across the moors towards Horton, Endon and Leek.

Any cart leaving the area bound for Leek or Rushton once used Hot Lane, which was little wider than the cart itself and served a number of farms and farm cottages. Some time before 1820, New Road - now Rudyard Road - had been put through, thus relieving Hot Lane of much of its traffic.

Bateman and Cooke's romantic vision of the moors was fashionable at the time. Queen Victoria's rose-tinted view of the untamed Scottish Highlands inspired travellers to head north, and Emily Bronte's *Wuthering Heights*, written three years before Biddulph Moor school opened, introduced its readers to Heathcliffe and his moors, both romantically brooding with a healthy dose of melancholy thrown in.

Cooke would lower the windows of Bateman's brougham at Wickenstones and enthuse over the intricacies of the wind-etched rocks, while Bateman's wife would wax lyrical over the moorland ferns she'd gathered along the way.

Any romantic notions the Moor's residents might have had were tempered by harsh reality. Hostile weather, cramped houses, reliance on well-water, candles and oil lamps, the poverty of the area, the struggle to feed large families, the necessity to grow and rear much of what was eaten, the difficulty in leaving the moor, particularly in winter (even if you were a collier and your livelihood depended on it), the lack of sanitation - all these gave rise to a rugged, self-reliant people who were less concerned with rock formations than staying alive. Those seeking the consolation of a Sunday Service joined the growing Methodist church. The rest were put off making the journey to St Lawrence's in the valley, where an hour's trek awaited their return home.

Competition for souls

In James Bateman's view, the Church of England had neglected such isolated communities as Biddulph Moor, Harriseahead and Mow Cop. A devout churchman, he felt it his duty to make Anglican worship available to all. He was not oblivious to the impracticality of attending services at St Lawrence's, Biddulph, or St Michael's,

Horton, two churches of long-standing separated from the moor by arduous walking across hilly terrain. He was also aware that lack of an orthodox church had left a vacuum which the non-conformists had been happy to fill.

The Wesleyan Methodists had been active in the area since the end of the 18th century; John Wesley himself had stayed at the house of a local convert. And now Hugh Bourne's and William Clowes' potent brand of 'Primitive' Methodism had gained a toe-hold in the area, with open-air preachers descending on Bailey's Hill and the rocky outcrops beyond his father's deer park at Knypersley. They were attracting crowds and practising conversions wherever a piece of uncultivated land could be found.

It had only taken Hugh Bourne three days in 1815 to raise the money for a Methodist chapel at the Cloud, and three weeks to build it. In 1852, as the National School at Biddulph Moor received its first scholars, a Primitive Methodist chapel opened its doors at Under-the-Hill. True, if the people hadn't come flocking, allowances had been made to convert it into a couple of houses. But they had, and it was in use for more than fifty years until its replacement in a more central location.

Then there was the Wesleyan chapel, built in 1818 at Beckfield's and active until 1886, when it was dismantled, some of the stone used in the façade of the adjoining house, but most reused in the far grander New Road Methodist Church which was under construction in 1887.

Methodism was grabbing souls and gaining strength not only on the moor but in working communities in all parts of the country. Clearly, the moor was ripe for salvation. The blessings of an ordered, spiritual and civilised life were the right of every man. And Bateman intended to reach both man, woman and child through the strength of the Church of England; his church, the church of monarch and state.

He'd made a start when he built the school. Children would be the first beneficiaries of the Church of England's moral compass. He'd seen to it that a schoolroom was registered for Sunday worship, though this was only a stop-gap measure. He'd already built a temporary parsonage for the curate who officiated at the services. But the schoolroom was cramped and lacked spiritual dignity. And the capacity.

Once the money had been raised, he'd give the moorland folk a church to be proud of. Simple, yet commanding. Plain, but inviting, modern and well-proportioned. Cooke's early sketches had been of an ambitious Italianate building, a far cry from the gothic chapel John Bateman had built at Red Cross. The final, more modest, result would still be a church to draw glances - and, hopefully, large congregations.

Religious services were held at the National School (1852) until funds for the church could be raised.

3. BATEMAN'S DILEMMA

Bateman was an impatient man. No sooner had he and his father completed the church and school at Red Cross than he had Biddulph Moor firmly in his sights. His plan was for a school and church to occupy a central location within the developing village. The overall responsibility for the project would be his, from quarrying stone to soliciting funds for the buildings. Though Edward Cooke had made preliminary sketches of the temporary parsonage and the church, his future activities would be confined to the Grange gardens, which would occupy much of his energy over the next thirteen years.

From early 1850, Biddulph Moor church and school had also absorbed much of Bateman's time. The small parsonage would be adequate for the curates who would work under the direction of William Holt, Vicar of St Lawrence. It was conveniently situated close to the Grange, Holt's vicarage, Elmhurst, (1841) and the village. When the church had been built, Bateman would erect a more fitting parsonage close by, and sell the smaller building.

In June, Bateman had made a profit of £550 (£632 before commission) from the London auction of rare orchids he'd grown in his father's Knypersley hot-houses.

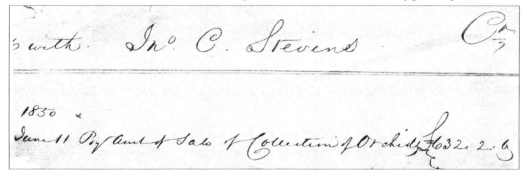

Bateman's orchids were sold through London auctioneer Stevens for £632.2.6d (before commission). The money raised went towards the cost of the temporary parsonage at the Hurst.

He'd already decided to put at least some of the money towards the cost of the small parsonage before going off with Cooke to celebrate with a dinner of turtle and a firework display at Surrey Gardens.

He saw school and church as symbiotic. They would complement each other and each was essential if his work was to succeed. Children had to know right from wrong, and to be instructed in the Biblical teaching which the church would provide and which would inform the way they lived their lives. But which should come first?

Church or school?

Churches were springing up everywhere in an attempt to accommodate a surging population and in the hope that, with God on side, the revolutions raging in Europe would get no further than the Channel. Some churches were being enlarged or undergoing insensitive restorations advertised by those seeking to bring them back to their more devout medieval roots and sweep away whatever had been built since.

On the other hand, the scholars of today were the parishioners of tomorrow.

Parishioners and children enjoying a Sunday-School and choir outing to the sea-side. Late 1940s

Funding for both church and school was not without difficulty, though he would contribute and grants and other subscriptions would need to be found. But the cost of erecting two buildings at the same time was a tall order, particularly as his gardens were devouring money and far from complete.

His dilemma was compounded by the recent availability of a defunct silk mill in the Hurst. He considered converting the buildings into a school, church and parson's house. On the other hand, would a converted mill be a viable proposition? Though it was closer to the moor than the Biddulph church, parishioners and children would still have to trudge over half a mile to get there, and scholars would have to make the journey at least twice a day if they weren't helping with harvest. The road was rough, narrow and steep. An icy winter would empty pew and desk alike.

His misgivings were echoed by the Revd Crawford Antrobus of Eaton Hall and patron of St Michael's Church at Horton, with whom Bateman had corresponded regarding the silk mill site. On July 23rd, 1850, Antrobus wrote: 'Your [proposed] church and Biddulph Church seem fully to supply the wants of the valley, and if we could plant churches as readily as trees, I should be prepared to join in having the silk mill as a third place of worship on the lower ground. But I feel the situation would do no good to the population of the upper part of the moor. The children would not go down to that school nor the adults to the service. A clergyman should be placed in the middle of the moor to be useful to the population there.'

By the following month, Bateman had discarded the idea and opted to proceed with a church and school in the central location he'd originally envisaged. This time the Revd Antrobus was enthusiastic, writing on August 5th: 'I think your present plan a great improvement on the old one... if you will accept a small subscription from me, I will tender £30 towards your undertaking'. Other contributions followed, together with an offer in September by Captain Mainwaring of Whitmore Hall to allow stone to be mined from his quarry on Bailey's Hill free of charge.

Revd J Brierley of Mossley Hall, Congleton, promises £50 (about £25,000 today) towards the church shortly after the committee's meeting in June, 1860.

By 1851, Bateman had concluded that the first building to be erected must be the school, and a committee was formed to work with him in attracting grants and subscriptions to see the project through to completion. His decision was also influenced by the possibility of licensing the school for Sunday worship until such a time as the church could be built. As the Bishop of Lichfield wrote in January, 1852: 'I cannot doubt that the friends of the [proposed] church in your neighbourhood have judged wisely in directing their beneficial exertions for the present to the providing of schools, while the prospect of a church and a parsonage at a future time will not be put out of sight'.

The Revd Enoch Trees

Bateman's busy life had encouraged his talent for delegation, and the Revd Enoch Trees was charged with steering the school through its early stages. In

Bateman's letter to Mainwaring bore fruit. The latter generously agreed to provide stone free for the school and later, the church, from his quarry on Bailey's Hill.

BELOW:
Revd Trees, initially in charge of BM school, was busy ordering stock a few months after the school opened. Note the slates and the lead pencils.

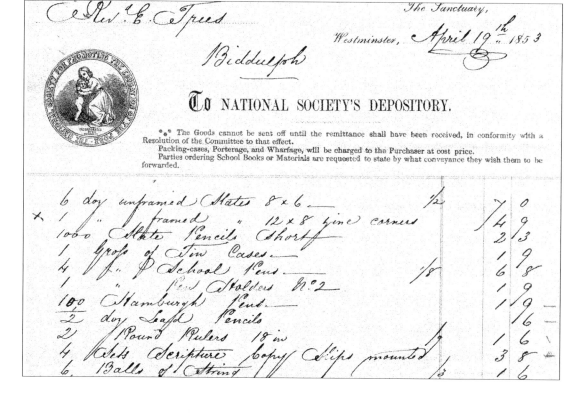

The 1861 census shows curate Francis Gordon and his wife Elizabeth living at Moor Parsonage, Hurst. The 'full sized' parsonage by the church was built two years later. Bateman and his wife were born in Sussex.

1851, Bateman appointed a Mr Lockett to try his hand at a plan for the school which would be acceptable to the education boards in London and Lichfield - bodies that were in a position to offer grants towards new school buildings.

These, along with money raised by charitable individuals, would also pay the wages of teachers and the purchase of stock. The Rev Trees had his time cut out ploughing through the financial intricacies of grant provision for the school, at the same time seeking funding for the proposed church through charitable bodies such as the Corden Fund, which itself was affiliated to the Lichfield Diocesan Church Extension Society.

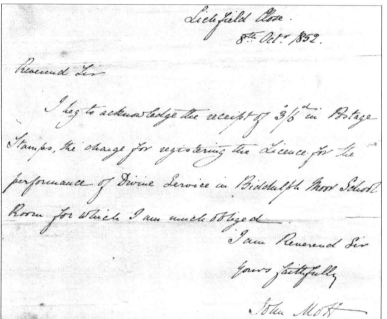

Revd Enoch Trees was delegated to arrange a temporary licence for divine services at BM school until the church was built. The fee was met in postage stamps.

He became sufficiently conversant with the financing of what was the novelty of educational provision, that we still find him ordering school supplies (6 doz. unframed slates, 1000 slate pencils, 4 gross school pens, 2 doz. millboards) from the National Society for Promoting the Education of the Poor in the Principles of the Established Church in April 1853, five months after the first scholars filed through the doors.

It was also up to Trees to procure a Licence for the Performance of Divine Worship from the church authorities in Lichfield Close. This he did in October, 1852, a month before the school opened. The charge for obtaining the licence was 3/6d, and it had to be paid promptly, in postage stamps.

As the school moved to completion, building began on the small parsonage in the Hurst. By 1854 it was ready for the first of the curates who would be responsible for religious duties in the now licensed school, and, if everything went according to plan, the church. The first curate, Revd Weston, moved in with his wife in 1855. He was followed a few years later by the Revd Clark and, in 1860, by Revd Francis Gordon.

Francis Gordon would become the first incumbent of Christ Church, and, in due course, rector.

Revd Francis Gordon, curate, then rector, of Christ Church 1863 to 1884.

4. A CHURCH FOR THE MOOR

Polite society in 1860 was still reeling from the claims made by Darwin in his *On the Origin of Species*, published the previous year. The church itself was thrown into turmoil over the question of evolution. Some church men considered a text which reduced God to no more than a bystander in the evolutionary process blasphemous and wicked.

A debate on evolution was due to take place in Oxford on 30th June, 1860. Cooke and Bateman, who'd arrived in Oxford the day before, had bought tickets to attend. The meeting was sure to be heated, with Darwin's combative 'bulldog', Thomas Huxley, taking up Darwin's cause and the church's case being met by the equally eloquent Samuel Wilberforce, Bishop of Oxford.

Though the debate would be overshadowed later that year by the first instalment of Dicken's *Great Expectations* and the launch of the world's first iron-clad warship,

Darwin's controversial *On the Origin of Species*, published a year before the first meeting of the Church Building Committee, was another catalyst to the building of the church.

HMS Warrior, it would add urgency to Bateman's unfinished business of a church for the moor; the church was as much a testimony to the strength of Bateman's religious conviction as the Geological Gallery he'd built at Biddulph Grange.

There could be no better time to start the project. The school was receiving excellent reports from the inspectors, the curates had already done sound work in the area and now the new curate, the Revd Francis Gordon, had arrived from Sussex with his wife, Elizabeth, and was settled in Hurst Parsonage. His reputation for what the Victorians called 'usefulness' had convinced Bateman that he was the man to see the church through to completion, just as the Revd Trees had assumed initial responsibility for the school.

The first meeting

At 12 noon on 5th June, 1860, the Biddulph Moor Church Building Committee met for the first time in Bateman's study at Biddulph Grange. Besides Bateman, who was unanimously elected Chairman, four ministers were present: vicar of St Lawrence, the Revd William Holt, the Revd Francis Gordon, the Revd W Melland, vicar of Rushton Spencer, and the Revd W Sutcliffe, of Bosley Parsonage. Two influential laymen were also present: John and Richard Myatt, both from Higher Overton.

Bateman was called upon to outline the progress of the Biddulph Moor Church Building Scheme to the present date. This was followed by a discussion regarding the best way of 'executing this much needed church for the moor'. The church at the time

A late 40s photo of the ladies of the Mothers' Union taken outside the old school while three of their children look (warily) on.

Part of the minutes of the first formal meeting of the BM Church Building Committee, June 5th, 1860.

found the word 'money' indelicate and innumerable euphemisms were employed in its place. In this case, 'executing' meant raising cash, and a lot of it.

The conclusion was that the neighbourhood be canvassed for funds, that application for aid should be made to the Church Building and Diocesan Societies, and that letters should be sent to the 'undermentioned' individuals. That the 'undermentioned' comprised wealthy locals who mixed in Bateman's circle will come as no surprise. Among those solicited were Samuel Pearson of Lawton Hall and Hugh Henshall Williamson of Greenway Bank Hall.

A treasurer was necessary at this point. Again, Bateman was elected, while Francis Gordon offered his services as Secretary. Two further items were announced before the close of the meeting: first, that four subscriptions to kick the project off had already been received; Lord Egerton of Tatton, (Bateman's wife Maria was of the Egerton family) and Mrs Stanier of Madeley Manor had each donated £100, Thomas Rowley, a London-based gentleman, £30 and the Revd Melland 5 guineas. (a labourer of the time earned around £12 a year) Second, that a sub-committee be appointed to make 'arrangements and enquiries' for carrying out the scheme. Unsurprisingly, Bateman volunteered, along with the Revd Gordon. Bateman's uncle the Revd William Holt, and John Myatt were also co-opted.

The sub-committee couldn't be accused of inefficiency. In less than a fortnight, Hugh Henshall-Williamson had donated £50 towards the church, and a few days later a surprise subscription of £25, sent in Bank of England notes, was donated by a Mr Ainsworth, of Moss Bank, Bolton.

Others were more hesitant, having already subscribed to church building in other parishes. One such was the Revd James Brierley of Mosley

The Sunday School group with their teachers in the late 1960s.

Hall, who wrote an apologetic letter to Francis Gordon on 25th June: 'I am well aware there are few places which require a church more than the moor. My heart is willing enough to help you more, but my purse is a very limited one. This year it is quite out of the question giving you any portion of the £50 [I promised] and I should much prefer only giving you £25 next year if this be spared and the remainder the succeeding year.'

The Lord Bishop of Lichfield, who also considered a church for the moor 'to be one of special urgency' put his name down for £10, while noting the 'considerable help' the project could receive from the Diocesan Church Extension Society in Lichfield and the Incorporated Church Building Society in London, and furnished Francis Gordon with the names and addresses of their respective secretaries

Grants and funding

The Bishop's letter hinted that his job was to collect donations and distribute grants, rather than provide them from his own pocket. Furnishing Bateman with the names and addresses of the various societies was irrelevant, since Bateman had had the information to hand since at least 1850. On the other hand, the Bishop was inundated with requests for funding the huge number of proposed churches in his diocese, and the information he gave was provided to a wide range of church builders, some less conversant with grant provision than others.

Grants then underpinned the building of schools, parsonages and churches, raised through donations and benefactions and distributed through various societies. In the case of schools built before 1870 - after which the ratepayer-funded boards took over - those who wished to build a school typically applied to the National Society for Promoting the Education of the Poor in the Principles of the Established Church. Hence the 'National' school, of which the school on Biddulph Moor was one.

Where churches were concerned, grants were available from societies working within the all-powerful umbrella of the Ecclesiastical Commissioners, set up in 1840. The sub-committee charged with 'making applications for aid to the Church Building and Diocesan Societies' first contacted Charles Gresley, the Secretary of the Lichfield Diocesan Church Extension Society. This society relied in part on revenue drawn from a bequest provided in the will of one Edward Corden Esq, and grants could be made if the applicant was able to provide sufficient security in land, buildings or cash and provided acceptable answers to the questions on the provided form.

For example: What is the name of the place on behalf of which the application is made? What is the population for which the new church is intended? What number of sittings is the proposed church intended to provide for Adults and for Children? What is the estimated expense of erecting the church? Has a grant been made by the diocesan committee? How soon is it expected to be finished if the funds can be made?

The other body to which the committee's attention was drawn was the Incorporated Church Building Society, based in London. The society's request for information made similar claims on the sub-committee's time - particularly Francis Gordon's, to whom much of its correspondence was directed.

The sub-committee was also charged with 'canvassing the neighbourhood for funds'. Bearing in mind the people of the moor, like many working communities in the country, struggled to make ends meet, their contribution was modest. Nevertheless, without their involvement in distributing advertisements, selling tickets for money-raising ventures, collecting money for visits to Grange Gardens and attending to the myriad essential tasks involved in fund-raising, the project would have been delayed and the people it was intended to serve, neglected. The same commitment was evident in their raising large sums for Hospital Saturday, fifty years later.

Whether the farm labourer's mite or the gentry's cheque, the receipts in the church account opened by treasurer James Bateman at the Manchester and Liverpool District Bank in Congleton continued to grow.

Ward and Son

The Building Committee entrusted the drawing up of formal church plans to Hanley architects Ward and Son, (Ward and Son and Ford from March, 1862) who had been involved in the designs of other churches and who were conversant with the exacting requirements of church societies. Working drawings and specifications based upon the much-modified version of Bateman's and Cooke's initial concept were supplied shortly after the first meeting of the Biddulph Moor Church Building Committee. Then, on 19th February, 1861, an estimate of the costs involved were sent to Bateman. These included £50 for the ground, £700 for the building and £450 for 'fitting up and

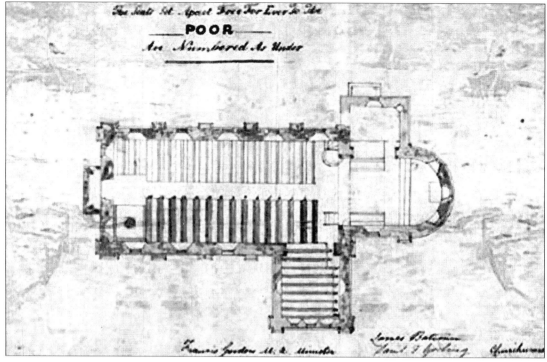

The Seats Set Apart Free For Ever To The
POOR
Are Numbered As Under

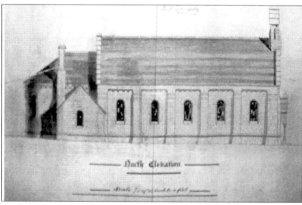

Ward and Son's plan of the church interior.
The poor of the parish occupied the free
dark pews, while children sat on benches
in the transept.

Left
The North elevation

fencing'. This made a total of £1200. Ward also acknowledged that their estimate was 'full, so as to influence the societies to offer a more generous grant'.

From February 1860 until June the following year, Ward and Son corresponded with Francis Gordon on an almost weekly basis. Gordon had taken over the day-to-day business of liaising with the architect, the church authorities, Bateman, the Building Committee and sponsors - as well as delivering Sunday Services in the school room.

The architects were equally demanding, politely yet firmly cajoling the hard-pressed Revd Gordon to send back their site plans and the plans showing the intended position of the church, and to send off for the relevant forms from the Lichfield Diocese Church Extension Society and the Incorporated Church Building Society which they themselves would complete to improve grant eligibility. They made it clear that the Ecclesiastical Commissioners would not countenance the building of any church if plans and paperwork were missing or incomplete.

Perhaps Francis Gordon was slower to respond than they hoped, and they misconstrued his tardiness for a reluctance to comply with the streamers of red-tape coming his way. His letter from Ward and Son on 18th February complains: 'Their [the Church Society] regulations are very arbitrary, but it is no use attempting to resist them, for unless the plans and other documents are in order, they will certainly send them back... It will save trouble in the end if you will be good enough to send us the plans and specifications by return in order that they may be put strictly in order and the particulars sent with them properly filled in'.

Ward also cautioned against Gordon's sending plans back to Lichfield directly 'as that society will require one or two detailed drawings and our specification was only sent you in rough draft for examination'.

By August, precise plans had been drawn up. But there were still niggles. Ward and Son were aware that the church societies would require half of the pews to be 'free' as a condition of a grant. The other half would be 'appropriated' (rented by any better-off parishioners with the money raised going towards church maintenance and the minister's wage). Would Gordon discuss this requirement with Bateman before asking the societies for their forms and sending them to Ward and Son to complete?

It was eventually decided that the side nearest the pulpit would be 'appropriated', and the other side 'free'. All this took time, and although in October 1861 Bateman gave instructions to Ward and Son for the updated plans and forms to be sent on to the Lichfield Diocesan Society, they arrived too late (and still incomplete) for the society's autumn meeting and wouldn't now be looked at until December.

Amendments were duly made. These included revised estimates of cost, with the intention of posting them off by November 15th in plenty of time for the December meeting and with a prayerful 'We now think [the plans] are so orthodox that you can surely have no difficulty in getting through with them'.

But the Revd Francis Gordon was still dragging his heels over the question of the cost of the transept intended to accommodate Sunday School scholars and other children. Ward provided yet another amended plan, advising Gordon that the transept they had drawn could be shortened to lessen the cost, but doing so would reduce the accommodation to fewer than the 100 child-places Gordon had envisaged. They also suggested shaving more money from the project by shortening the chancel and vicar's vestry while introducing a separate door in the transept for the children to use.

Gordon conferred with Bateman, who wanted the chancel and vestry to remain as planned but accepted the idea of a reduced transept. He also queried the need for it to have windows. Ward and Sons countered that the windows would provide useful light and cost no more than a solid wall.

The latest adjustments were made. Ward and Son sent the documents, plans and forms back to the Lichfield Diocesan Society in time for the December meeting. On 31st December 1861, the architect sent a note to the Revd Gordon to say they were 'grateful to hear' the plans have 'at last passed the Lichfield Society with so little alteration'.

Once this had been attended to, the plans would go to the Incorporated Church Society in London, which would 'affix their seal' before sending them back to Francis Gordon. By spring, 1862, tenders for building the church had been advertised.

Ladies of the Mothers' Union (now the Ladies' Fellowship) seem delighted with their visit to Champion Bakeries in this late 1950s photo.

Rector Revd Geraint James (1958-65) receives his leaving gift of a mantel clock from long-term choir member Percy Mitchell of Rock End in 1965.

5. VYING FOR TRADE

Ward and Son had a reputation for reliability and their dealings with the Biddulph Moor Church Building Committee were always professional, on more than one occasion pre-empting the requirements of the church societies. Bateman was impressed by their knowledge in preparing and revising the church plans, and had drawn £25 from the Building Committee's account to meet the architects' fee.

Meetings
Bateman announced at the Building Society meeting on 11th February, 1862, that the total raised now stood at £607. 3s - £100.7s of which had been paid to the treasurer's account in the Manchester and Liverpool District Bank. A grant of £200 had also now been offered by the Lichfield Church Building Society.

A mood of growing optimism prompted Bateman's decision to 'start as soon as could be, and to advertise for sealed tenders for the work at the earliest date'. Advertisements were to be placed in the papers, with a line to inform potential builders that copies of the plans and specifications would be available in Hurst Parsonage and at Ward and Son. Copies from Ward could also be obtained for 5/- a time. Responses to advertisements were to be posted to Revd Francis Gordon.

The advertisements were carried by the *Macclesfield Courier and Herald* and *The Staffordshire Advertiser* on 15th February, 1862. The former newspaper, owned by James Swinnerton, charged £5.6d for the entry; *The Staffordshire Advertiser*, which boasted a weekly circulation of 10,000 copies, charged a more modest 3/6d.

The plans were to be held in the parsonage from the date of the advertisement until the end of the month, and the short time span generated a flurry of activity among local contractors. By the time of the Building Society's 11th March meeting, a list of interested parties already lay on Francis Gordon's desk.

Tenders
Nine tenders had been received., ranging from £895 to £1325. (Ward's estimate had been £1200) Only two builders - Cephas Cottrell and Joseph Stanway - were local. Of the rest, one was from Bradley Green, one from Burslem, one from Wetley Rocks, and three from Hanley. Other addresses were not given. All were keen on the work and used to building in stone.

Messrs Cottrell and Brown, who were willing to do the job for £1220, suggested that 'if the committee thinks proper to alter anything so as to reduce the price, [we are] willing to leave the price to Messrs Ward and Son, architect, Hanley'. The Bradley Green builder, John Harding, quoted a figure of £1200 for 'hammer and dressed' and twenty pounds less for 'zig-zag and dressed'. Burslem builder John Woolwich was willing to take on the work for £1191.10s ' perhaps he thought the extra ten shillings would clinch the deal by convincing the committee of his precision in practical matters, adding '.... if my tender should meet with the approbation of the gentlemen concerned, I shall do my best to give every satisfaction'.

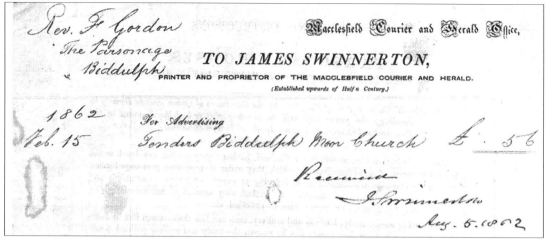

The Staffordshire Advertiser and the Macclesfield Courier and Herald enjoyed wide circulation. Francis Gordon was delegated to invite tenders for building the church through their columns. The Macclesfield proprietor received the Building Society's cheque six months after the ad was placed.

Henry Goldstraw of Wetley Rocks tendered £1345, whereas Cephas Cottrell submitted a figure of £956.10s on the basis of 'plain work according to Mr Gordon's instructions, viz. No bell, plain vestry screen, plain communion table, no ribbed groins in the windows and all hammer-dressed stone for walling'.

Hanley builder Edward Matthews quoted £1260, and Joseph Stanway £1120.10s. Stanway's was the most detailed of all the applications and is worth quoting here:

'Gentlemen, the following is my tender for building, erecting and finishing the new Church at Biddulph Moor according to the plans and specifications prepared by Messrs Ward and Son and Ford of Hanley. Viz: for excavating, draining, getting the stone, carting, stone masonry, building, tiling, providing lime and sand, bricklaying, plastering, carpentry and joiners' work, plumbing, iron-work, bell and fittings and all other works agreeable to the intent and meaning of the said plans and specifications for the sum of £1120.10s. Witness my hand this eighth day of March, one thousand eight hundred and sixty two.' Joseph Stanway, Biddulph Moor.

Securities

The Building Committee's meeting of March 11th, 1862, also stipulated that the chosen contractor deposit a security of £250 to be forfeited if the work was left incomplete or deficient. It was considered a wise precaution to make enquiries into the viability of those offering the two lowest tenders, and to ascertain if they were able to offer securities. If they couldn't, the next lowest tender able to offer the necessary sum was to be accepted and the work begun immediately. The conditions were met by Joseph Stanway and he was given the job.

On 3rd April, 1862, an official agreement was drawn up between Bateman and the builder, authorising the penalties involved if the work was not completed on time.

The Incorporated Society

The announcement on March 11th that a further grant of £175 would be forthcoming, this time from the Incorporated Society for the Building of Churches, was good news.

But there was devil in the detail. Ward had been in touch with the society since January, and it was no less zealous in raising procedural points than the Lichfield Society. Contingent upon their offer of a grant was a request to supply a drawing showing the number and siting of the pews, accompanied by the church plans and a copy of the diocesan surveyor's report. These were duly sent.

The accommodation of children in the transept was a particular sticking point, and Ward, probably in answer to the Incorporated Society's query, modified the seating to include backs to the children's benches. In a note to Gordon, they explained: '.... forms are not so well for young children when they have to sit for several hours without any support for the back'. And, as a sop to the committee's relentless drive to keep down costs, added: 'The boarding of the pews might be left out for economy and made to consist of rails and elbows only'.

Further minor quibbles included the cost of a slate versus tiled roof. Ward preferred locally manufactured tiles, declaring '...slates will cost rather less, but the difference will be a mere trifle'. The committee eventually went for the patterned blue tiles which figure widely in Victorian churches, hotels and station-masters' houses. Ward and Son and Ford also wrote that a plain stone pulpit rather than a wooden one might save a few coppers, but the committee disregarded the suggestion.

Ward was more assertive when it came to building materials, insisting that Astbury lime be used for all walling and Froghall lime for all plastering. In fact, the architects were a guiding light on the requirements of the church societies and construction work, and their advice, passed through Francis Gordon, was invaluable to the smooth progression of the project. Bearing in mind the poor state of roads at the time, staff made the

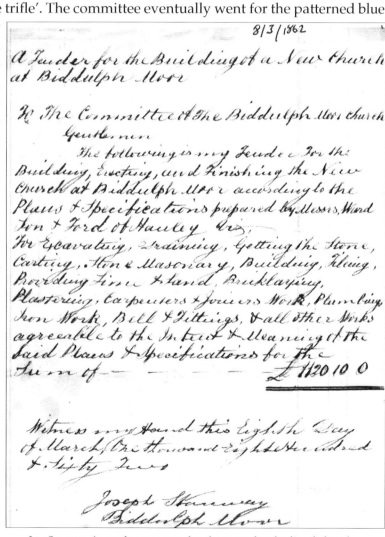

Joe Stanway's tender was not the cheapest, but he lived close by and was able to offer the security demanded by Bateman.

Plant sales have long been a popular method of church fund-raising. Revd McGuire (left) and his wife Margaret (left of table) seem pleased with the result in this 1980s picture taken outside his Rectory.

Revd Ian Stephenson (1965-9) presides over a party of young parishioners in this late 1960s picture.

journey from their Hanley office to Biddulph Moor in all weathers to examine the quarries on Bailey's Hill from which stone would be extracted, providing estimates of the quantities needed and which beds would provide the best results.

Subscriptions

Though by April 1862 the building was underway, Francis Gordon was still worried about the amount of money needed, and voiced his concerns to Ward. On 25th April, the architect sent him a sympathetic letter: 'I am sorry to hear you are still so much deficient in the funds for the church, but know well that clergymen must always anticipate somewhat in such matters if they must do the good they are appointed to do. I shall be willing to give both you and Mr Bateman all the assistance in our power at the most moderate charge. I shall be in your direction next week and will call and look at what Stanway is doing as a matter of importance, that he should start right with the building.'

The first tranche of money wasn't due to Joseph Stanway until May. In the meantime, there were other unavoidable costs which, though modest, mounted up. For example, printing circulars and writing accompanying letters to potential subscribers; with postage and advertisements for tenders, all had to be met from funds received.

As the summer of 1862 approached and the building work progressed, outlay extended to bazaars, entrance tickets to Grange Gardens and sock-knitting by ladies just as anxious as James Bateman to continue the good work and bring in the money.

And they were persuasive. Over the course of 1862, the total amount raised would reach £1412.11.1d. Contributions given or promised were written in the Biddulph Moor Church Building Fund booklet, whose pages record offerings made by the wealthy and the not so wealthy in meticulous detail: Lord Egerton of Tatton, £100, Mrs Stanier of Madeley Manor, £100, Rev J Brierley of Mossley Hall, £50, Hugh Henshall Williamson, of Greenway Bank, £50, Miss Sparrow of Bishton Hall, £20, Mrs Kinnersley of Clough Hall, £10, S F Gosling of Lea House, £10 and others.

Not everyone on the lists was a household name. Numerous local well-wishers with a limited purse but a stout heart contributed their mite, and if they were unable to do that, gave of their time and talent. A Miss Wathen produced an altar cloth for sale, £2 was raised from refreshments sold in Grange Gardens, Thomas Brassington gave £1, a Mrs Metcalf collected £1.13.6d from neighbours, and a Mrs Dudfield raised 14/10d at a Mothers' Meeting in London.

The pressure to raise money has a contemporary ring to it. Both Bateman and Gordon were well aware that costs wouldn't stop with the building of the church. There would still be the undrained church yard and its walls to attend to and a repair fund to set up. That was apart from the costs involved in acquiring the site. In the meantime the building work went on.

Far from Biddulph Moor, Victor Hugo, exiled on Guernsey, published the first part of his epic novel *Les Miserables* on the day Joseph Stanway signed his agreement with James Bateman. Two weeks later, Louis Pasteur invented pasteurisation. The American Civil War, which would claim 750,000 lives before it ended in 1865, rumbled on. And Christina Rossetti published her famous poem *Remember* as the fund-raisers of Biddulph Moor knocked on doors, baked cakes, offered tea and sold tickets.

The Revd Ian Stephenson (1965-69) with the church choir, early 1960s. The processional cross was given in memory of long-serving churchwarden, Charles Elkin.

A church outing, possibly late 50s although the coach is earlier - perhaps to Trentham Gardens. Bill Hall, the bus owner is on the left. Bill's son, stooping, front left.

The Anniversary Sermon was a popular church event when this 1950s photograph was taken.

BELOW
The Bishop of Lichfield (Revd James appears to be holding the crozier) attends this early 1960s confirmation gathering following the service.

6. AGREEMENTS AND SPECIFICATIONS

The agreement

By the end of summer, 1862, the church was well underway. Carts made daily journeys from quarry to site; each load added to the next course. A large team of local masons and labourers worked ten hours a day, six days a week.

Joseph Stanway was in charge of all employees, and their wages were made out from the sums allocated to him through the Building Committee. This was paid in stages in either cash or cheques by James Bateman, and consisted of varying amounts depending on the progress of the work and the vagaries of the weather. In May he received his first £30, followed in June by two payments of £50 and £60. The following month he was paid two sums of £100 and £50. £50 was receipted in August, and again in September, with a further £100 the following month.

Stanway couldn't help but be mindful of the small print in his official contract, drawn up with Bateman on the 3rd of April, which laid down strict penalties if the execution of the project was not pursued in a 'substantial and workmanlike manner', and that 'he had to effectively and duly complete the whole of the works required.... in the erection and finishing a new church at Biddulph Moor.' He was also obliged to proceed only in strict accordance with the 'plans, sections, working drawings, elevations and specifications proposed by Ward and Son and Ford, architects'.

The man in the foreground has been identified as Arthur Craig, a long-time church member who always sat on the back pew.

These were not unreasonable safeguards, albeit written in a legally-binding document. And the requirement that he provide and deliver 'all bricks, stone, timber, tiles, slates, lead and iron and other materials' arguably carried fewer risks than the stipulation to 'roof and cover [the building] before the first day of November [1862] and to complete the whole building and works before 1st April the following year'.

The penalties for failure to do so were explicit. He would be obliged to forfeit £5 for every week the buildings remained uncovered, and £10 for every week after April 1st, 1863, that the church remained incomplete. The money would be deducted from his bill by Bateman, and the work would only be considered complete on certification by Ward and Son and Ford. But there was a rider: should Bateman require 'additional works to be done or cause the works to be delayed', the additional time would be allowed to Stanway for roofing in or completion.

Thus Joseph Stanway was allowed little room for manoeuvre - and it didn't stop there. If Ward decided that the workforce, the quality of work or the materials were deficient, they were authorised to give the builder written instructions to sack men and to remove defective materials from the site. On the other hand, if in the architects' opinion too few men or too small a quantity of materials and tools were available to meet the conditions laid out in the agreement, they were to demand in writing that Stanway rectify the situation forthwith.

If he did not comply within seven days, Bateman reserved a statutory obligation to dismiss the builder and employ another to finish the job. The new builder's fee would then be deducted from Stanway's tender of £1120.10s and Stanway paid off 28 days after the architects certified the church complete - less £100, which would be retained by Bateman as a security against the 'failure of any portion of the works for 12 months after the issue of a completion certificate'. Furthermore, Bateman was entitled to any stone and other materials which had been carted to the site but remained unused.

Specifications

Ward's specifications for the church were produced in a 9 page document which also included site plans, elevations, cross and longitudinal sections and a detailed drawing of the roof structure. They carry trade headings - excavator, bricklayer, stonemason, tiler, carpenter, joiner, plasterer. Information for plumbers, glaziers and painters was given in a single section, with a brief note to ironfounders ending the document.

Excavators

The excavators were instructed to spread material dug to accommodate the building neatly around the area. This was presumably in readiness for levelling the site, which fell towards Church Lane and which was later enclosed in the retaining wall we see today. The deepest excavation was the 'firing vault', which was to be built under the vestry to house the 'heating apparatus'. Excavators also had to lay a 6" drain ready to take water from the roofs and the firing vault to the nearest outlets.

Masons and bricklayers

Bricklayers were to build an arched firing vault 7ft high from 9" brickwork, using hard-fired blue bricks. Both bricklayers and masons had to use a mortar of one part Astbury lime to 2 parts of sharp sand from neighbouring sand pits throughout the building. The stone, procured from the best beds at Bailey's hill, was to be 'hammer-dressed' with ashlar work [squared stone masonry and thin blocks of dressed stone for facing brickwork] neatly tooled.

Low under-floor walls were to be constructed to carry the oak sleepers supporting 1"thick red deal floorboards on which the pews would rest. Solid tooled stone would be used for steps and entrances, set on a mortared bed of rammed stone

Plasterer

The walls inside to be rendered floated and trowelled in haired mortar

The ceilings to be lathed rendered floated and set in plaster between the rafters - the laths to be nailed to the diagonal rafters and to be of the strength called lath and half

To point stop and make good all damaged places at the completion

The mouldings to doors and window openings to be run in gauged plaster

The walls and ceilings to be tinted by mixing the finishing coat with coloured sand and the moulds and arches to be coloured stone colour

The lime used to be from Froghall and the sand to be from the neighbouring sand pits

Ward and Son produced comprehensive hand-written specifications for each trade employed in the building of the church.

Agreement

made this Third day of April in the year of our Lord One thousand eight hundred and sixty two Between the Reverend James Bateman Esq. of Biddulph in the County of Stafford of the one part and Joseph Stanway of the same place Builder of the other part

The said Joseph Stanway for the considerations herein mentioned doth hereby for himself his Executors or Administrators Contract and agree with the said James Bateman that he the said Joseph Stanway his Executors or Administrators shall & will at his & their own proper costs & charges do & execute in a substantial & workman like manner effectually & duly the whole of the works required to be done in the Erection & Finishing a new Church at Biddulph Moor in the County of Stafford according to the Plans Sections & Working Drawings Elevations & Specification prepared for the purpose by Ward Son & Ford architects in the County of Stafford for the Price or Sum of Eleven Hundred & Twenty Pounds Ten Shillings of lawful money of Great Britain and shall & will at the like Costs & Charges provide & deliver all the bricks Stone Timber Tiles Slates Lead Iron and all other materials required for or in and about the said Works & Buildings of the several qualities dimensions & descriptions mentioned in the said Specifications and subject to the Conditions & Stipulations contained herein and to roof & cover in the same on or before the First Day of November next

Part of the agreement to build the church drawn up between Bateman and Stanway on 3rd April 1862. It outlines the penalties put in place if the building is not roofed over and completed in time. See p.32

and bricks 'broken small'.

A $^3/_8$"damp course of Stockholm Tar and tallow, poured hot, and external gratings to ventilate the sub-floor were specified. The minister's vestry would have the luxury of an open coal fire, and a 14" by 10" flue would take smoke from both the vestry and the firing vault. The minister's hearth and chimney would be of stone, and a 'College' grate costing 8/- would complete the fireplace.

The stone font would contain a 23" diameter basin, 13"deep and lined with 7lb lead, with a $1^1/_2$" hole to take unused water into the drain. The font was to be stabilised using dowels sunk into the polished step on which it would stand. Masons would also be required to make channels in the window jambs, sills and arches to receive the leaded lights, and perforations to carry condensed moisture outside.

Tilers, carpenters, joiners

The best blue plain and ornamental tiles for the roof and ornamental ridge tiles were specified, with tiles for roof valleys made to accommodate the pitch.

The carpenter was to use Baltic timber for the roof, and the joiners well-seasoned Petersburg or Archangel deal free of large knots. Oak pins would join the roofing timbers, the latter planed and chamfered wherever they were able to be seen. Wrought iron spikes were specified to attach the rafters to the wall plates, and the dimensions of all roof timbers were laid down - including 1" by $^5/_8$" tiling laths, which had to be fixed to the rafters using wrought iron nails dipped in boiled linseed oil to help prevent rusting. There was a further instruction: to stain all exposed roof beams in dark oak and to treat them with two coats of the best copal varnish.

Closer to the ground, carpenters were obliged to make the pews of 2" thick deal. At 2'9" from floor to their moulded capping, they had to accommodate 13" wide seats and be firmly fixed to the joists. On the other hand, a seat width of only 9" was considered adequate for the children's benches in the transept, and the railed back support recommended by Ward had to be provided.

Instructions for making the communion rail with 'a portion in the centre being hung as a gate.... with hinges and a brass flush bolt to fasten it with' were given, as well as a 'good plain table for the chancel, with a 2" top moulded round the outer edge.' The design of the pulpit was equally specific; it was to be made from $2^1/_2$" thick framing and contain a 'projecting book board supported on brackets'. Neither were the pulpit steps left to the whim of the carpenter; each tread had to be $1^1/_4$" thick, and the hand-rail a substantial $4^1/_2$" by $2^3/_4$" - presumably to withstand the grasp of passions yet to be raised during one hour sermons.

A novel ornamentation would be the moulded screen separating the chancel and vestry, with its 'arcade of turned shaft-moulded arches' and a vestry door 'formed in it, hung with brass hinges and having an ornamental latch'. Against this screen, the original organ was to be set, and is likely to have remained in place until the more ambitious pipe organ was later introduced under the transept.

No vestry is complete without a capacious cupboard. The one provided by the joiners was 6ft high and 3ft 6" wide and has been in situ since 1863. Another task for the joiners was to erect the necessary timber work to support the 56lb bell destined for the bell-turret, together with ropes and pulleys and a 'piece of copper tube through the roof for the rope to work in'.

Plasterers, plumbers, glaziers, ironfounders

The inside walls of the church were to be rendered, floated and troweled in haired mortar and the ceilings lathed, rendered, floated and set in plaster between the rafters. The plaster for both was to be tinted by mixing 'coloured sand' with the finishing plaster coat. Plaster for mouldings and arches was to be 'coloured stone colour'; the lime used in the plaster was to be sourced from Froghall and the sand from 'neighbouring sand pits'.

Plumbers were contracted to use 5lb lead in flashings between the chancel and nave, and 6lb lead under the end of ridge tiles and the apex of the apse.

The glazing for the windows was specified as 'good seconds crown glass' in diamond patterns, secured to wrought iron stay bars with lead ties. The glaziers were cautioned to immerse the window lights in 'oil cement for six weeks before being fixed to the opening'. Once in place, they were to be pointed in cement, with all ironwork connected to the windows given two coats of red lead and two of oil paint in a 'plain colour'.

The ironfounders' time would be largely taken in making cast iron guttering and downspouts, which were to be fixed to the wall with wrought-iron brackets.

By the 1st of November, 1862, the roof was on. But that didn't mean subscribers could rest on their laurels....

The sale of work in this 1974 picture went towards the restoration of the pipe organ,
which was dismantled for rebuilding in 2011.

GRANTS AND SUBSCRIPTIONS

TO THE

BIDDULPH MOOR CHURCH

BUILDING & ENDOWMENT FUNDS

UP TO DECEMBER, 1862.

	£	s.	d.
James Bateman, Esq., for Endowment Fund	1000	0	0
The Lichfield Church Building Society, for Building Fund	200	0	0
The Incorporated Church Building Society, for ditto	175	0	0
Proceeds of Biddulph Moor Church Bazaar	132	6	9
Proceeds of the Grange Garden Tickets at the Biddulph Volunteer Review	104	12	0
The Rt. Hon. Lord Egerton of Tatton	100	0	0
Mrs. Stanier, Madely Manor, Newcastle-under Lyme	100	0	0
Rev. J. Brierley, Mossley Hall, Congleton	50	0	0
H. H. Williamson, Esq., Greenway Bank, Tunstall	50	0	0
T. Rowley, Esq., London	30	0	0
W. H. Ainsworth, Esq., Moss Bank, Bolton	25	0	0
Miss Sparrow, Bishton Hall, Rageley	20	0	0
Rev. J. Brierley, (2nd donation)	20	0	0
Proceeds of Mow Cop Bazaar	20	0	0
The Lord Bishop of Lichfield	10	0	0
Rev. Francis Gordon, Moor Parsonage	10	0	0
Mrs. Kinnersley, Clough Hall, Kidsgrove	10	0	0
Miss Wathen, Biddulph Grange	10	0	0
S. F. Gosling, Esq., Lea House, Biddulph	10	0	0
J. B. Thorpe, Esq., Manchester	10	0	0
Collected on Moor Church Ground at Commemoration Meeting	9	0	0
Sermon at Biddulph Parish Church	5	11	5
Rev. W. Melland, Rushton Parsonage	5	5	0
Mr. Yardley, Rushton Spencer	5	0	0
R. Wilbraham, Esq., Rode Heath	5	0	0
Rev. S. Bradshaw, Basford Hall, Leek	5	0	0
Mr. R. Myott, Higher Overton, Biddulph	5	0	0
— R. Myott, Lower Overton, Biddulph	5	0	0
Rev. W. Foster, Horton Parsonage, Leek	5	0	0
A Friend, by Mrs. Bateman, Biddulph Grange	5	0	0
R. Sewell, Esq., Manchester	5	0	0
Late Miss Frances Sewell, Manchester	5	0	0
G. H. Ackers, Esq., Moreton Hall	5	0	0
Sermon at Horton Church, Leek	3	0	0
Miss Selby, Biddulph Grange	2	2	0
Mess. Warrington & Sheldon, Congleton	2	2	0
Charles Harris, Esq., London	2	2	0
Mrs. Thorpe, London	2	0	0
Mr. Goode, Congleton	2	0	0
Mrs. Hutton, Congleton	2	0	0
Messrs. Miles and Brunt, London	1	10	0
Mr. Burghope, Congleton	1	1	0
— Webb, Congleton	1	1	0
Captain Jones, R.N., London	1	1	0
Two Friends, London	1	0	0
Rev. M. Brock, Bath	1	0	0
Mr. Woolley, Congleton	1	0	0
Messrs. Aston, Congleton	1	0	0
Mr. Braddock, by Mrs. Myott, Higher Overton	1	0	0
Thomas Livsey, Esq., London	1	0	0
George Livsey, Esq., London	1	0	0
Francis Merritt, Esq., London	1	0	0
Joseph Kimpton, Esq., London	1	0	0

Building doesn't come cheap. The extract names some of the subscribers and their donations in order of size.

7. SUBSCRIPTIONS, AND COLLECTIONS

The sums raised up to the end of 1862 were many, some were substantial, and a list of contributors was published by the Building Committee in December. Gifts by fellow clergy should come as no surprise, since many were gentlemen of independent means who came from well-to-do families. The names of some local vicars have already been given, but the list shows a wider subscription base, with offerings from a Revd Brock of Bath, the Revd Foster of Horton, the Revd Bradshaw of Basford Hall, Leek, and even a Revd Arthy of Bognor.

Other subscribers gave a London address, and were probably friends of Bateman, who shared similar scientific and horticultural interests and frequented such clubs as the Athenaeum. Money was also donated by Bateman's family. His daughter Catherine gave 2/6d, (equivalent to three day's work for a labourer) and his sons Robert and Rowland £1 0s 6d each. William Holt's daughter raised £1, and he received £1 from Frank Wilbraham of Rode Hall. (Bateman's son, John, married into the Wilbraham family).

Neither was the Building Committee averse to enticing money from the businesses which had supplied the materials used in the construction of the church. Plumber, glazier, painter and paperhanger Joseph Delves, of Bradley Green, was roped in for 2/6d, and even Congleton stationer, bookseller and newsagent William Burghope, no doubt mindful of future calls on his service, parted with a guinea.

Small but significant collections continued to be made by committed locals. Given Bateman's flair for delegation, it wasn't long before the masters in charge of the schools on Biddulph Moor and Red Cross were co-opted to do their bit. Joseph Hall, who lived at School House on the moor raised £5.17s from eighteen villagers, some of whom bore the still-familiar surnames of Plant, Sherratt, Harvey, Clowes and Brassington. Mr Walton, of Red Cross School, raised £4.15s 8d (with a 5s contribution from himself) from the Baileys, Doorbars and Brooks' on his doorstep.

Even so, the ladies eclipsed the men, drawing on the modest purses of well-wishers from Knypersley, Bradley Green and Biddulph Moor to add £50 to the proceeds.

Fund-raising events
Life in mid-Victorian Britain was hard. Outings, gatherings, fairs, bazaars, pubs, home amusements and visits made a break from harsh routines and provided a bit of fun. They could also be turned to the Building Committee's advantage.

Bazaars, for example, attracted large crowds then much as do car boot sales now, and more than one was organised for the benefit of the church programme. Not all took place in the vicinity - one, at Mow Cop, raised a creditable £20. But those held at Biddulph Moor did even better. On 19th August, 1862, a sizeable £73 was made on the first day, with a further £35 a week later. A third bazaar, on September 1st, turned a profit of £11.1s.5d. Tickets to view Grange Gardens were also sold, (with light refreshments) raising £17.8s.6d, making a total of £136.9s.11d. altogether.

Tickets to Mr Bateman's gardens never failed to attract the curious and those whose brush with ornamental plants was limited. The sale of tickets at the bazaar of 28th August brought in just over £104, and those passing through his Geological Gallery and glimpsing the wonders beyond were more than willing to pay the small amount asked for the experience.

There were overheads. The cost of printing tickets, circulars and posters advertising events was normally put through printer and newsagent William Burghope's Congleton office. Garden tickets were produced in batches of 100, each batch costing just over £2, and Burghope printed 600 tea party and bazaar tickets for the summer activities.

Then there were costs involved in the setting out of tables and chairs, as detailed in the bill for 12/6d presented to Francis Gordon by Edwin Sherratt for the bazaar on the 19th August. The hire of crockery at £1.14.3d for each of the three bazaars was an another expenditure.

The adage 'the workman is worthy of his hire' was never so apt as in Victorian England, where a rate of labour charges was laid down for every activity - even pumping the bellows of a church organ or setting out tables for a bazaar. And such activities were sometimes coupled with more adventurous events. A case in point is the bazaar of 28th August, where side shows included a demonstration by the Biddulph Volunteers (Rifles). Although this raised the overall profits to more than £104, a fee of £3 had to be met for the hire of tents from the Norton Floral Society.

The Pathfinder class, 1970.

Another method of contributing money was through collections given following a sermon in aid of the church. £5.11.5d was raised at St Lawrence's in this way, and double that in a commemoration meeting later held at 'moor church ground'.

Tradesmen's bills

Bills dropped with alarming frequency through treasurer James Bateman's ornate letterbox; the bills addressed to Francis Gordon also found their way to the Grange.

These could range from railway freight charges to the purchase of brooms and lamps. For example, the church bell was transported by the North Staffordshire Railway Company from Birmingham to Congleton Station and hence to Biddulph Moor on November 14th, 1862, for a cartage of 1/-, based on its weight of 2qrs 13lb.

The bell was previously supplied in October and returned to the foundry of George

Transporting the church bell from Birmingham to Congleton sidings was a shilling.
In this instance, Bateman was the addressee.

Dowler of Birmingham as being unsatisfactory. It was mislaid in transit before being rediscovered, repaired and returned to Biddulph Moor.

The bill was paid through Bateman, as was £1 10 4d for a consignment of Holland cloth, cotton braid, tape cord, bobbins, thread, needles and diapers ordered in July 1862 by Mrs Gordon from Congleton haberdashers W H Aston. The materials were in readiness for use in the finished church as kneelers, altar cloth and choir vestments.

The heating system, supplied by ironfounder W Hancock of Fenton, was a greater drain on the committee's resources. Bateman received the firm's quote of £52 on the 29th July. For this, the church would get a wrought iron saddle boiler with feed cistern, underwork, two pipes across the chancel covered with a cast iron ornamental grating, two rows of 3" pipes along each wall of the nave, two rows of 3" pipes in the transept and all necessary air pipes. The cost included delivery to Biddulph Moor, but didn't allow for any brickwork and excavation which might be required. There was no mention of radiators in the estimate, but there was a promise to send 'Henry tomorrow with the pipes to your [Bateman's] house, when he will be able to give you any further information you require'.

Henry's journey by horse and cart proved fruitful, for Hancock's got the job - but not until the committee had knocked them down by £2. Bateman signed a £50 cheque on 1st January, 1863.

Another local supplier, owner of Biddulph Forge, Samuel Gosling, sent 237 best fire bricks on 8th December, 1862, and a socket shovel in early January the following year. The cost was £1.11.2d. Since the firing vault had been completed in the late spring of 1862, and the vestry chimney in early summer, it's possible the fire bricks were supplied in readiness for the new parsonage in Hot Lane, which would be built the following year.

Thankfully, such payments lay outside Joseph Stanway's remit. He also avoided the penalties which would have been imposed had not the church been roofed in by November 1st. Work now continued apace on the interior, and, with luck, completion by the following spring.

The Revd Ian Stephenson accompanies the Mothers' Union outing, mid 60s.

Fenton

Staffordshire

July 29th 1862

W. HANCOCK & SON,
IRONFOUNDERS, ENGINEERS,
AND MACHINISTS.

James Bateman Esq

Sir,

We beg to inform you that a wrot iron saddle boile with feed cistern, underwork &c, two pipes across the Chancel, covered with a cast iron ornamental grating, two rows of 3in. pipes along each wall of the nave, an two rows of 3in. pipes in the transept, all necessa air pipes, the whole delivered and fixed at Biddu Moor Church will cost £52 — This amount is exclusive of all brickwork and excavation.

We will send Henry to-morrow with the pip for your house, when he will able to give you any further information you may require.

Yrs obediently

W Hancock & Son

Ironfounders W Hancock and Son of Fenton offered to install the church's heating system for £52.

8. AN END IN SIGHT

The winter of 1862/3 was mild, with typical temperatures above freezing throughout much of the country. This was welcome news. A severe winter would play havoc with the schedule, materials would have remained undelivered in railway sidings and workers from outlying areas would have struggled to reach the site. The American Civil War showed no sign of ending, and the birth of three men destined to make their mark - David Lloyd George, Henry Royce and Frank Hornby - went unnoticed amid the rasp of sawn timber and the swish of the plasterer's float.

Joe Stanway had his fingers crossed and an eye on the calendar. The same was true of the Revd Gordon, who had enough on his plate guiding the project through its final stages and liaising with ecclesiastical societies, tradesmen, solicitors, suppliers, the Building Committee and the often elusive James Bateman.

Even after Stanway's April 1st deadline had been met and the church was technically functional, some items would still warrant attention. Tradesman Thomas Chadwick got the bell to work smoothly, provided a stained wooden rail for a vestry curtain, fixed skirting in the transept and completed a communion table for £2.2.0d. He also made 'tablets' for the church, which took six and a half days, employing two men to fix them to the wall before finding them unsatisfactory and taking them back to be altered. Once they were up, he set about producing an oak-stained vestry table.

William Burghope was now receiving orders for hymn books and posters advertising the forthcoming consecration. Shopkeeper James Webb of Buglawton sent brooms, brushes, mops, scouring flannels and a 1/6d galvanised bucket, while in Bradley Green Joseph Delves made out an itemised bill of £21.11.1d for sending men to paint the bell swing, fix the lightening conductor, add extra downspouts and number the pews in black.

The pace was hotting up. The forthcoming consecration, May 28th, was on everyone's lips. The Lord Bishop of Lichfield would be there. Everything had to be perfect for the day. The newly-quarried grit-stone building was already a landmark in the village.

Bateman seemed to have invoked the clause in Stanway's agreement which allowed extra time if Bateman required 'additional works to be done', since he didn't receive his final payment of £25.14.11d until November 23rd, 1864.

Bateman's excursions

James Bateman wasn't averse to responsibility, and his prowess at delegation has already been commented on. The installation of influential locals to his committees would have been relatively straight-forward for a wealthy coalmaster who'd married into old Cheshire money, and his reliance on curate Francis Gordon to oversee the church while keeping an eye on the school gave him freedom to pursue his interests.

In this he was no different to other well-heeled Victorians with enthusiasms to indulge. Once building began in April, 1862, we find him and Maria in St James' Hall, London, listening to Charles Dickens acting out the dialogue between Squeers and

1863 Revd H Jorden   Dr
              To Thos Chadwick

May 4 To Tablets for Church
       To 32 ft 1½ inch Red deal   8 0
       To Glue & Screws   8
       To Coskerham 6½ days at Makeing
       the tablets   1 10 4
       To two men 1 Day each at fixing
       the tablets in Church   9 0
       To two Notice Boards in Porch
       at Church and Fixing them and
       6 hold facts Painted over 6 times   11 6
       To Vestry table Stained with dark
       Oak & Varnished drawer & Lock
       on it   18 0
       To Loss by takeing the first
       Tablets back again   15 0
                                          £ 4 " 12 " 6

       Jany 25 1864
       [stamp ONE PENNY]

Chadwick's of Bradley Green were still busy with internal fixtures a few weeks before the church's consecration. This bill of May 4th, 1863, wasn't paid until the following year.

Nicholas Nickleby. This was followed by dinner at the Royal Academy.

Two months later the Batemans were again in London, visiting the Roman and Egyptian Courts at the Great Exhibition. January 1863, found him attending a lecture on the radiation of heat through the Earth's atmosphere at London's Royal Institute, and the following month visiting the Athenaeum. Even in early May, as the final preparations for the consecration were being made, he found time to take the London train from Congleton to discuss with Cooke his [Bateman's] plans for Oxford Park, in which he was involved. He caught a late train back to Congleton, leaving Cooke and his sisters to make their way to Covent Garden for a performance of Verdi's *La Traviata.*

The consecration of the church failed to curb his appetite for the metropolis. No sooner had it taken place than he was back in Town, visiting the National Club and accompanying Cooke to Covent Garden to see *The Barber of Seville.*

It was only in August, when Cooke spent a fortnight at the Grange before one of his jaunts to France and Italy, that Bateman stayed put for a few weeks. And even this brief respite was broken when he and his estate workers spent a couple of days digging around the ruins of Biddulph Old Hall to see what they could find.

The consecration

The consecration of Christ Church was a seminal event in Biddulph Moor history, and Thursday 28th May was etched in Bateman's calendar for 1863. Leaflets had been issued, posters distributed, the press informed. The church had been swept, the pews waxed and polished, the path to the door freshly gravelled to receive the first congregation and the ecclesiastical heavyweights brought in to lead the service.

Three tons of coal and slack were carted to the firing vault in case the weather took a turn for the worse, a choir had been produced and a celebratory lunch laid on (with beer). Service sheets had been provided by William Fell at the Bishop's office in Lichfield.

At the appointed time, John, Bishop of Lichfield, arrived in his landau. Flanked by the Revd Gordon and other clergy, his party processed to the crowded nave. From now on, services would no longer be held in the classroom but in the church- though Sunday Schools would continue there for some years and find an echo in the 'Parish Room' still used for church meetings at the time of writing.

After consecration

There were two services on the day of consecration, with collections raising £49.8.4d and £8.7.1d respectively. No doubt some of the children attending the morning service with the school would have been supplied with a halfpenny to contribute. The size of the initial collection signified the attendance of the well-to-do and a full church. Two services held the following Sunday raised a much reduced total of £10.4.8d. This could point to a fall-off in number - or the absence of those with greater resources, some of whom had travelled a distance to attend the opening ceremony.

Even a dignified event such as a consecration could present an opportunity for more secular pleasures. Grange Gardens were again opened to the public between services, and on this occasion visitors were treated to a multi-coloured riot of

(C) Christ Church — Biddulph Moor

Expences of Consecration of Church and Churchyard

		£	s	d
1863 Jan'y 1st	Retaining fee		5	6
	Perusing Deed of Conveyance of land &c and making Extract therefrom in order to draw a petition to the Bishop to consecrate a new Church and Churchyard at Biddulph Moor		13	4
	Drawing a list of queries and transmitting same for answers to enable me to draw the petition		13	4
	Perusing the answers and making Extracts therefrom		3	4
	Drawing Petition accordingly 36 Folios at 1/	1	16	-
	Settling and engrossing same and parchmt	1	5	-
	Transmitting same for signature with instructions Letter and postage		5	4
	The Petition having been duly signed attending the Bishops Registry therewith and praying same to be registered		6	8
	Paid Registrars fees		4	8
	Drawing and settling Deed of Consecration	2	2	-
	Engrossing same and parchment	1	10	6
	Paid Bishops Secretary for Episcopal Seal thereto	1	1	-
May 28t	Registrars fees for attending at Consecration	3	3	-
	Paid Bishop's Apparitor's fee	1	1	-
	Paid travelling and other expences of Bishops apparitor	1	16	7
	Paid Mr Fells travelling expences		18	-
		£17	5	3

The consecration was a costly endeavour, as is apparent from this extract.

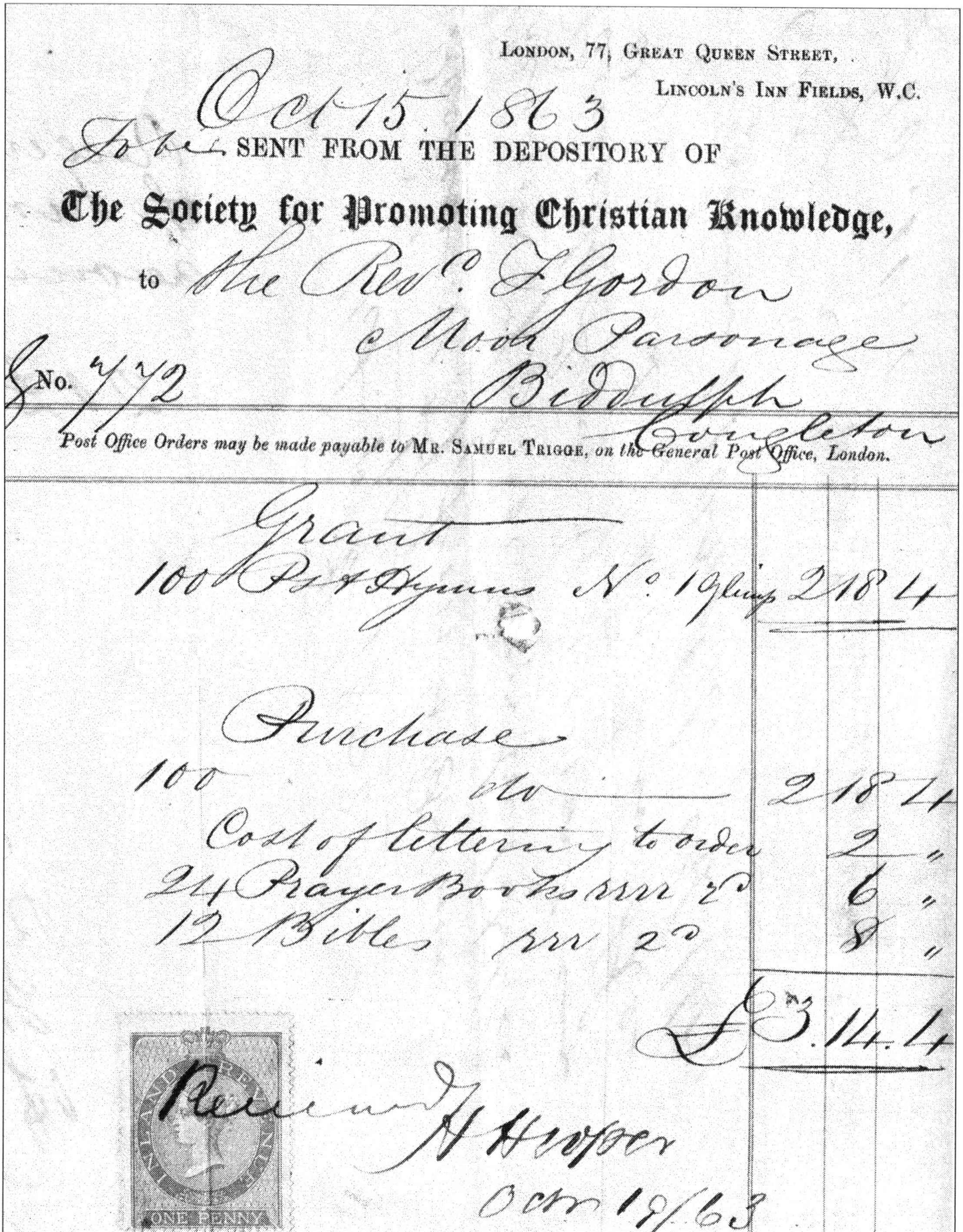

LONDON, 77, GREAT QUEEN STREET,
LINCOLN'S INN FIELDS, W.C.

Oct 15. 1863

To be SENT FROM THE DEPOSITORY OF

The Society for Promoting Christian Knowledge,

to *the Rev.d F Gordon*
Moor Parsonage
Biddulph
Congleton

No. *772*

Post Office Orders may be made payable to MR. SAMUEL TRIGGE, on the General Post Office, London.

Grant
100 Pet Hymns N.o 19 bing 2 18 4

Purchase
100　　　　　do　　　　　2 18 4
Cost of lettering to order　　2 "
24 Prayer Books xxxx 2.o　　6 "
12 Bibles　　xxx 2.o　　8 "

£3. 14. 4

Received H Hooper
Oct 19/63

Five months after consecration, Gordon was still arranging payment of bills. The London-based society supplying hymn books, prayer books and Bibles received payment within four days.

rhododendron blossom, followed by refreshments.

If the Revd Gordon hoped bills, fund-raising and supervising the site were a thing of the past, and he could now get on with running the church and superintending the school, he faced an awkward truth: Joseph Stanway was now engaged in making alterations to the new, full-sized parsonage in course of erection in Hot Lane, and would shortly be building 169 yards of churchyard walls intended to stabilise the large amount of spoil dug from the site. Moreover, Church Lane was still unmade, and carter William Bailey was busy delivering stone to the site and making up the road in June - a job which took him three days.

Meanwhile, Ward and Son and Ford continued to acquaint Gordon with the vagaries of taxation. In a letter of 8th July, 1863, they referred him to the customs' practice of allowing a drawback of duty used in the construction of churches 'on a proper declaration of the quantities used'. This could amount to as much as £12, and Ward offered to make the 'needful calculations and declarations which will be well worth a couple of guineas as our charge'.

They were, however, reliant on Joseph Stanway to produce the quantities, and he was in no hurry to respond to their plea that 'your early attention to this will oblige', with an exasperated 'we shall be glad if you will be good enough to reply to the questions as they are set down' thrown in. Ward was still waiting for Stanway to get in touch in late November, five months after the church's consecration.

And the bills showed no signs of easing. Prayer books, Bibles and hymn books from the Society for Promoting Christian Knowledge, a box of books weighing 2qrs 16lbs transported by the North Staffordshire Railway Company, lamps from Bradley Green dealer John Baddiley in readiness for services on dull winter days - all had a bill attached. And since lamps were of little use without oil, an order was placed with local druggist John A Williams for a supply at 3/- a gallon. The first consignment had been used by December 30th and re-orders were placed throughout January and February of 1864. Two months later the bill for fire insurance arrived from the Royal Insurance Company agent at Bradley Green.

However, the last winter order for 4 gallons of lamp oil was small beer compared to the costs incurred in the May consecration. After paying the registrar's fees, a deed of consecration, travelling expenses, letters of correspondence and a lengthy list of other items, a bill of £23.13.5d was presented to the Building Committee, which would find itself likely to be raising money into the foreseeable future.

Supplying the music

The question of the provision of music in the first years of the church is unclear. The plans produced by Ward and Sons refer to an organ to be located in the chancel against the vicar's vestry. The allocated space would have been insufficient for any but a modest instrument, such as a pedal harmonium, through no evidence survives for this and music could have been temporarily supplied by local instrumentalists if the envisaged organ failed to materialise.

What is certain is that a choir was formed from the time of the church's consecration, and it is unlikely their efforts would not have been supported by an instrumental accompaniment of some sort.

A letter by organ-builder Thomas Wilkinson survives in the church archive, quoting £135 for offering to build a piped organ. This is dated 14th June, 1871. However, since this was to be a new organ and the subsequent church organs date to at least the first half of the 19th century, his offer doesn't seem to have been taken up.

However, a piped organ which pre-dated the building of the church was obtained at around this time. This could only be accommodated beneath the transept arch, effectively rendering the transept redundant for the accommodation of children and isolating it from the rest of the church. It is likely that all pews became 'free' around this time, and the children were seated in nave pews alongside their parents.

This organ was sold to New Road Methodist Church, probably around 1900. (Worship at New Road began in 1888, and for a few years an ensemble of local players provided the music.) It survives in situ at the time of writing.

At the same time another organ was acquired by Christ Church. This remained under the transept arch until 2011, when the cost of its maintenance became prohibitive and it was dismantled and transported to Kent by an organ enthusiast with a view to its rebuilding. Its place is now taken by a modern electric organ, most of the money for which was provided by the sale of the 'new' vicarage five years earlier.

The PCC in 1970. Revd John McGuire and his wife Margaret centre

The third church organ partly dismantled in 2011.

The second church organ found its way to New Road Methodist church, where it still is today

Taken in the church hall, late 1950s, this probably shows the opening of a Christmas Fair.

9. A PARISH OF ITS OWN

The mechanisms conferring legal status on the church were born of a labyrinthian process which delighted the Victorians but does nothing to ease the task of the contemporary researcher. Red tape and the pedantic observance of ecclesiastical small-print were the stock-in-trade of the commissioners who were the final arbiters on all matters to do with grants and finance, and teams of experts conversant with church law were on hand to prove it.

The letters pouring from the pens of the army of clerks working from their London headquarters in Whitehall Place were peppered with the vocabulary of their trade. Benefice, augmentation, enlargement, benefaction, cure, consolidated chapelry, endowment, engrossment and perpetual annuity spill across the lines of secretarial longhand and leave the reader in no doubt that they knew the rules of the game and it was up to you to learn them.

Christ Church might have been up-and-running, with congregations bursting with enthusiasm for this new sort of Sunday, but there was still much for Francis Gordon to do before the enterprise - not to mention his wage - was on a firm footing. Organising the building of the church was one thing; dealing with freehold tenure, the collection of rent-charges, the formation of an ecclesiastical district and his status within it was ongoing and delivered in an uncompromising tally of forms and letters which landed twice daily on his new hall tiles.

To each his due

The diocese of Lichfield, like all English diocese, was expected to work closely with the Ecclesiastical Commissioners in implementing church planning in their region. Communication between Francis Gordon, the Bishop of Lichfield and William Fell and Charles Gresley of Lichfield Close was frequent. It was to these latter that Gordon would turn in the first instance to answer any queries arising from endowments, patronage deeds and the costs involved in consecration.

The diocese also introduced a table of fees to be used in all churches: the minister was to receive 2/- for the service of burial of a parishioner, 10/6d for the erection of a headstone, £3 for a vault containing two coffins and 2/- for the publication of the banns of marriage. The sexton could also expect 1/- for an hour's tolling of the funeral bell, 4/- for digging a grave 6ft deep and another 1/- for each extra foot dug.

Nor was casual labour voluntary. Higham Sparling's surviving notes (he succeeded Revd Francis Gordon and was the incumbent at Christ Church until 1902) record payments made to locals employed in running the church from March to June, 1884: 'Cephas Cotterill paid 2/- for lighting fires in the minister's vestry and 13/- for ringing the bell for Sunday services.' 'Sarah Sutton earned 13/- for cleaning the church and 3/- for lighting the oil lamps on six evenings.' 'Carpenter Mr Booth received 7/6d for fixing curtain rails in the vestry, and Charles Plant 12/2d for carting coal.'

Thomas Goldstraw was variously engaged in firing the boiler, ringing the bell and pumping the organ, and attending to the minister's kitchen garden, for which he

Revd Higham Sparling succeeded Francis Gordon as rector 1884-1902. He was a keen amateur astronomer.

received 8/-, 13/- and 6/6d respectively. 4/5d was paid to schoolmaster and church organist Herbert Reeve for the purchase of scores, and a further £3.5.9d to Mr Booth, this time for unspecified repairs.

Higham Sparling's Lancashire background as a book-keeper and cotton waste dealer (as well as a member of the Royal Astronomical Society) also stood him in good stead when it came to dabbling in stocks and shares. This proved rewarding for both him and his congregation, enabling him to provide alms to the poor of the parish. Between March and June, 1884, he distributed sums to many parishioners who had fallen upon hard times. In his will (he died aged 76 in 1916) he bequeathed £100 to the people of the moor. This expired in 1921.

Buying the land

The Mainwarings of Whitmore had held land around Biddulph since the 16th century. The quarries on Bailey's Hill were owned by them, and the land where Christ Church came to be built was part of their estates. James Bateman and Admiral Mainwaring, in whom the Mainwaring estate was then vested, had entered into an unofficial agreement: Admiral Mainwaring would exchange the church site on the moor for a parcel of land of equal value owned by James Bateman.

There was a snag. In April, 1862, before this could be legally ratified, the Admiral inconveniently died. Notwithstanding his colourful military career (he was at the Battle of the Nile and the blockade of Copenhagen) and his three marriages - he was twice a widower - there was doubt whether his successors would agree to the arrangement.

What was to have been a simple transaction now looked less straightforward; the Admiral's son, Gordon, wouldn't move on the matter until he'd inspected the land and sought the approval of other interested parties involved in the Mainwaring estates.

By June, 1862, permission to exchange the land - and just as important, to convert it from leasehold to freehold - had still not been given. By July, the Mainwarings' solicitor, a Mr Broughton of Wistaston Hall, Nantwich, was involved. A letter from Charles Henry Mainwaring, Gordon Mainwaring's younger brother, wrote to Francis Gordon from Rhyl, where he was holidaying, to say there was 'some little hitch about the conveyance of the land. Our solicitor says we have no power to *give* the site, but that it may be managed in some other way. He proposes that you go over to him and give him full particulars and he will do all in his power to help you. It may be best to write and fix a time for seeing him. I have written to Mr Bateman to the same effect. I hope there will be no serious delay, but I think you had better see Mr Broughton.'

At the time, a return journey from Biddulph Moor to Nantwich would take all day. But it was essential the land was conveyed and the leasehold converted into freehold, since the ownership of property, including land, was necessary to secure the Commissioners' support. Francis Gordon made the journey on 29th July, 1862.

Luckily, his time wasn't wasted, for the following day the trustees of the Mainwaring family gave their assent to the church site as Admiral Mainwaring had agreed. On 18th August, Mr Broughton was instructed to draw up the Title of Freehold and to inform the Ecclesiastical Commissioners of the change in the land's status.

The conveyance of the land to James Bateman was made after much to-ing and fro-ing of letters to the commissioners, Lichfield, Broughton, the Mainwarings and Francis Gordon. The purchase of the lease amounted to £40, and the plea went out for hard-pressed subscribers to dig once more into their pockets. Fortunately, they did. The money was paid in January 1863; Broughton's bill was settled the following month

Church Choir with choirmaster Ken Sherratt, 1970.

Grants, endowments and benefactions

Grants supporting the building and operation of schools and churches were widely available during Bateman's time. But there were strings attached. The National Society for Promoting the Education of the Poor in the Principles of the Established Church, which gave rise to the so-called National Schools, would offer grants only if schools' inspections confirmed that an acceptable standard had been reached in terms of learning, teaching, financial soundness and organisation.

The Ecclesiastical Commissioners also expected something in return for their input into new churches. That something was cash or its equivalent in land, property, ('including parsonages') and other sources of revenue or investment. Funding in the form of grants, interest on money given and annuities to support the minister and maintain the church were usually offered in return for such benefactions.

An endowment was also offered by the patron of a new church. This was legally binding in order for a church to be consecrated. In the case of Christ Church, the patron, James Bateman, offered £1000 on 13th February, 1863 - well over half a million pounds in today's money - in readiness for the consecration three months later. The endowment was made through the office of the Bishop of Lichfield, and a bond was officially drawn up and ratified by Lichfield registrar William Fell.

Bateman also offered the commissioners £50pa raised through rent charges on his own land to provide curate Francis Gordon with a wage of the same amount, paid to him half-yearly. This was to be a temporary measure, until an ecclesiastical 'district', belonging to Christ Church, could be created.

Revd John McGuire and his wife, Margaret, shortly after his ministry began in 1971.
Revd McGuire was behind much of the upgrading of the church and church hall in the 1970s/80s.

Hard times

Gordon began his ministry as a curate working under St Lawrence's vicar William Holt. Christ Church had no distinct parish of its own, and when Gordon delivered a service of burial or baptism (he wasn't licensed to conduct the wedding ceremony until 1864) the fees were claimed by the Rev Holt as incumbent of the mother church. The modest £50 pa raised by Bateman to provide a temporary wage was hardly augmented by either pew rents or the collection plate. Gordon's response to a question raised in a form he returned to the Ecclesiastic Commissioners in October, 1864, makes his position clear: 'The inhabitants of the district are too poor to render any aid to [my] income. The incumbent's private means are next to nothing, and he feels the importance of a permanent income being settled as soon as possible.'

A permanent income, where he'd be entitled to fees from baptisms, burials, marriages and a rent charge levied on local farms under the tithe system (in which one tenth the value of such farms' produce would go to the church) would only come about if a specific district, or parish, were assigned to Christ Church, which would make it independent. The church was at present a chapel of ease - so called because it offered to local people the comfort, or ease, of not having to make the journey to St Lawrence's each Sunday. But it had no autonomous jurisdiction, and this was a concern to poorly-off curate Francis Gordon.

Creating a district

Autonomous districts were being formed all over England as the rapid growth in population led to the erection of numerous churches to meet the demand of those living

ECCLESIASTICAL COMMISSIONERS FOR ENGLAND.

Office ;—10, Whitehall Place, London, S.W.

File. No. *20626*

QUESTIONS to be answered by INCUMBENTS.

.*. It is *earnestly requested* that each of these Questions may be carefully, fully, and particularly answered.

1. What is the name of your Benefice or Church ?	*Christ Church Biddulph Moor*
2. Is it a Rectory, Vicarage, Perpetual Curacy, District Church, or Chapelry ?	*a Consolidated Chapelry*
3. In what County ?................. Diocese ?....................... Archdeaconry ?................ Deanry ?.................. and Parish ?................... and—What is the Post Town ?......	*Staffordshire* *Lichfield* *Stafford* *Leek* *Biddulph* *Congleton, Cheshire*
4. If not a Parish Church, has a District been legally assigned to your Church or Chapel ?	*a District legally assigned*
a. If so, state the names of the Parishes or Ecclesiastical District out of which such district was taken, and also the Act of Parliament under which the assignment was effected.	*The Parishes of Biddulph & Horton Act eighth & ninth years of Her majesty Cap. 70. and Act of nineteenth and twentieth of Her majesty Caps. 55. Lay Patronage*
5. In what Patronage is the cure ?	
a. If it be in the Patronage of any Rector, Vicar, or Perpetual Curate, as such, in what Patronage is the Rectory, Vicarage, or Perpetual Curacy ?	*James Bateman Esq. Biddulph Grange is the Patron of the Parish Church*
b. If it be a new Church or Chapel, now in the Patronage of any such Rector, Vicar, or Perpetual Curate, is it *permanently* so? if not, in whom will the Patronage eventually become vested ?	*The Patronage is permanently vested in James Bateman Esq.*
6. What is the area in statute acres of the Parish or District actually under your spiritual charge as Incumbent ? (If the exact acreage is not known the best approximate statement should be given.)	*Do not know the acreage - but the District is 3 miles long & 2 miles broad*
7. What is the Amount of Population (according to the last census) actually under your spiritual charge as Incumbent ?	*over 1200*
8. How many persons can your Church accommodate ?	*308*
a. What Number of the Sittings are free ?	*209*
9. Is there a Glebe House ?.................	*Yes*

This and the following extract are from the Ecclesiastical Commissioners to Francis Gordon.
He makes a plea for a 'permanent income' which will only come about when rectory status is granted.
Three days after he completed the form, the problem was resolved.

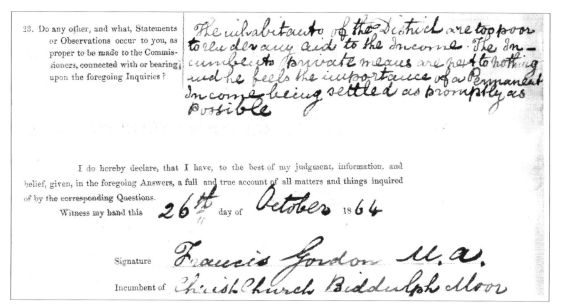

23. Do any other, and what, Statements or Observations occur to you, as proper to be made to the Commissioners, connected with or bearing upon the foregoing Inquiries?

The inhabitants of the District are too poor to render any aid to the Income. The Incumbents private means are next to nothing and he feels the importance of a Permanent Income being settled as promptly as Possible

I do hereby declare, that I have, to the best of my judgment, information, and belief, given, in the foregoing Answers, a full and true account of all matters and things inquired of by the corresponding Questions. Witness my hand this 26th day of October 1864

Signature *Francis Gordon M.A.*

Incumbent of *Christ Church Biddulph Moor*

on the edge of extensive parishes. In Biddulph Moor, Bateman had had in mind an eventual 'district' for more than a decade before the church was built. A letter to him from the Revd Crawford Antrobus dated July 23rd, 1850, refers to the (proposed) formation of a separate district, to be carved out of the Parish of Horton after the church's completion.

The Parish of Horton shared a boundary with that of Biddulph, and in the event it was intended a new district be created from a portion of both. This would be a time-consuming process necessitating the agreement of the vicars of St Michael's and St Lawrence's and the Ecclesiastical Commissioners, who wanted a further endowment of £150pa at the time of the district's formation. This sum would render the proposed district eligible for a grant, met from a common fund. Even so, a grant wouldn't be forthcoming until the population of a new district, its area and the needs of its parishioners had been taken into account.

Francis Gordon didn't pull his punches in stating the case for a district in a letter to the commissioners in April, 1863. He reminded them of the financial sacrifices Bateman had made in providing an income of £50 pa from one of his Biddulph farms, the new parsonage he was building in Hot Lane at an estimated cost of £1000 and the purchase of the site for £40. He urged that these generous acts should be strongly taken into account in forming an ecclesiastical district, so that 'all services of the church might be brought within the reach of these long-neglected poor of England's church'.

He reiterated the poverty of 'this outlying quarter of the Parish of Biddulph', adding that '....the 1200 very poor people residing upon it [were] utterly destitute of any school accommodation until 10 years ago, when Mr Bateman built a school and master's residence and obtained a license to use the room for divine worship.'

Despite his pleas, Gordon was informed that the assets he outlined were insufficient to generate an income of £150pa, which was the legal requirement for the constitution of a district, until the church had been consecrated and Bateman's endowment of £1000 had been taken into account.

A fortnight after consecration, the Revd Gordon duly provided answers to the points raised by the commissioners in the first of the forms relating to the formation of a new district. *What is the church's accommodation?* 99 seats rented, 209 free: total 308. *Whose are the fees for baptisms and burials?* They are at present claimed by the vicar of Biddulph. *Does the Bishop and the incumbents of parishes out of which the district is to be taken approve of the arrangement?* They do. *What will be the district's extent?* About 6mls by 2mls. *In whom is the patronage of the church at present invested?* James Bateman of Biddulph Grange. *Who will be patron of the new district?* James Bateman. *Is there a residence for the minister?* One now being built and ready for occupation at Michaelmas. [September 29th, 1863] *What is the amount of pew rents if all were let?* About £20....

By July, 1863, the Ecclesiastical Commissioners were 'willing to recommend to Her Majesty's Council that the contiguous portion of the Biddulph and Horton Parishes be formed into a consolidated chapelry (a district carved from more than one existing parish) and requested that Francis Gordon send them a map showing the new district with the boundary distinctly defined.' They also required 'a verbal description of the farms, lanes and places which lay on the new boundary.'

The verbal description didn't reach the commissioners until September, 1863, together with an assurance that once a district was assigned to the church, all the offices of the church, including marriage, could be carried out. October was taken up in queries by the commissioners regarding benefactions which would be offered in return for their support in assigning the new district, and the matter would be put to the commissioners board on the 12th of November.

The outcome of the meeting turned out to be favourable. By January 1864, the legalisation of the district had moved towards ratification by the Queen. In the London Gazette of 5th February, the result was made official: Biddulph Moor now had its own district. The commissioners sent a copy of the Gazette containing the item to Francis

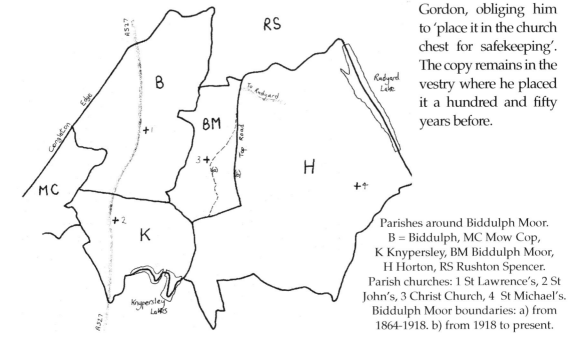

Gordon, obliging him to 'place it in the church chest for safekeeping'. The copy remains in the vestry where he placed it a hundred and fifty years before.

Parishes around Biddulph Moor. B = Biddulph, MC Mow Cop, K Knypersley, BM Biddulph Moor, H Horton, RS Rushton Spencer. Parish churches: 1 St Lawrence's, 2 St John's, 3 Christ Church, 4 St Michael's. Biddulph Moor boundaries: a) from 1864-1918. b) from 1918 to present.

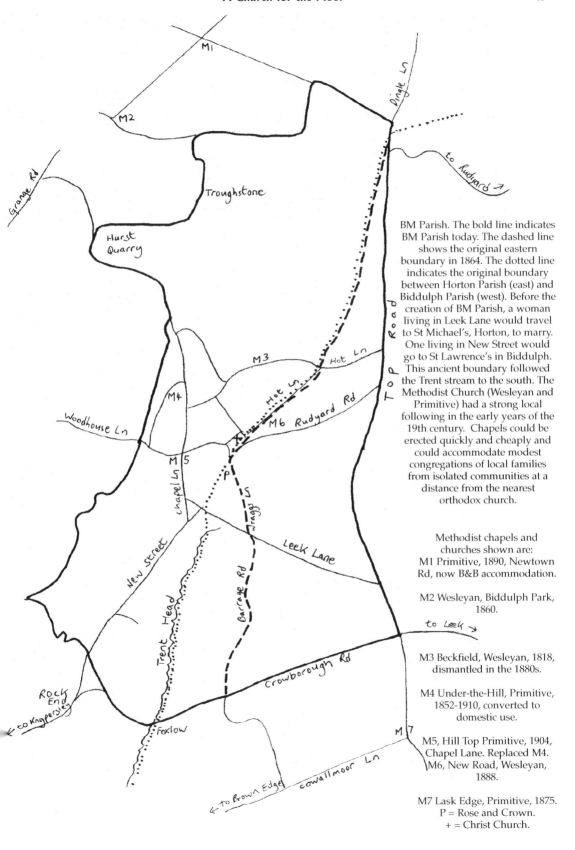

BM Parish. The bold line indicates BM Parish today. The dashed line shows the original eastern boundary in 1864. The dotted line indicates the original boundary between Horton Parish (east) and Biddulph Parish (west). Before the creation of BM Parish, a woman living in Leek Lane would travel to St Michael's, Horton, to marry. One living in New Street would go to St Lawrence's in Biddulph. This ancient boundary followed the Trent stream to the south. The Methodist Church (Wesleyan and Primitive) had a strong local following in the early years of the 19th century. Chapels could be erected quickly and cheaply and could accommodate modest congregations of local families from isolated communities at a distance from the nearest orthodox church.

Methodist chapels and churches shown are:
M1 Primitive, 1890, Newtown Rd, now B&B accommodation.

M2 Wesleyan, Biddulph Park, 1860.

M3 Beckfield, Wesleyan, 1818, dismantled in the 1880s.

M4 Under-the-Hill, Primitive, 1852-1910, converted to domestic use.

M5, Hill Top Primitive, 1904, Chapel Lane. Replaced M4.
M6, New Road, Wesleyan, 1888.

M7 Lask Edge, Primitive, 1875.
P = Rose and Crown.
+ = Christ Church.

From Chapelry to Rectory

At the end of April, 1864, a further £500 was raised in support of the new district and offered to the Ecclesiastical Commissioners. In return, the commissioners granted Francis Gordon a perpetual annuity of £16.13.4d to add to his income. The *London Gazette* published the figures and a copy was deposited in the church at the end of July.

The curate's position had improved, but his economic future would only be assured if the rent charge levied from the area, which now went to the patron James Bateman, could be claimed by him as a rector. It was important to him that this final stage in the church's evolution was completed at the earliest date.

On 14th October, 1864, Bateman offered the Ecclesiastical Commissioners the £50 rent charge his steward had collected in return for a grant from the common fund. It would be 17th March, 1866, before the commissioners accepted his benefaction, which would produce a grant to provide Gordon with a perpetual annuity of £41.13.4d once ratified in council and published in the London Gazette.

In May, 1866, Gordon was informed that the matter of converting the district into a rectory would be settled when the rent charge arising within the district had been legally attached to it. After further correspondence, he wrote to the commissioners giving details of the amounts of rent forthcoming from local farms and properties.

The total sum, together with the benefaction already offered to the commissioners, produced the result Francis Gordon had been awaiting: Christ Church became a rectory on 20th November, 1866, and was recorded in the London Gazette of that date. The designation 'rector' was to continue until the end of Revd John McGuire's ministry in 2001, when future incumbents would be designated 'vicars'.

First Biddulph Moor Girl Guide's camping equipment fund sale following their badge test in 1971. Examiner Hilary Williams, extreme right.

CHARITIES AND GIFTS TO CHRIST CHURCH BIDDULPH MOOR

THE REV. FRANCIS CORDON M.A. THE FIRST RECTOR OF THIS PARISH COLLECTED MOST OF THE MONEY FOR BUILDING THIS CHURCH WHICH WAS CONSECRATED IN 1863. HE GAVE £100 AS A FABRIC REPAIR FUND. AND BEQUEATHED £150 FOR A SUNDAY SCHOOL PRIZE FUND

THE RECTORY WAS BUILT IN 1863 THROUGH THE KINDNESS OF JAMES BATEMAN ESQ OF THE GRANGE BIDDULPH WHO ALSO GAVE £1000 TO THE ENDOWMENT FUND.

THE CHURCH SCHOOL WAS BUILT IN 1852 WHEN THE REV. E. TREES WAS CURATE IN CHARGE. IN 1885 THE SCHOOL WAS ENLARGED THROUGH THE KINDNESS OF ROBERT HEATH ESQ OF THE GRANGE BIDDULPH WHO ALSO PURCHASED THE GLEBE FOR THE BENIFICE AND GAVE THE CHOIR STALLS IN CHURCH.

IN 1916 THE REV. D. HIGHAM SPARLING B.A. BEQUEATHED £100 FOR THE POOR OF THE PARISH. IN 1921 THIS FUND EXPIRED.

IN 1920 JESSE MELLOR FORMERLY OF THIS PARISH LEFT £50 FOR CHURCH FUNDS

ROBERT HEATH Esq OF THE GRANGE BIDDULPH, WAS A GENEROUS BENEFACTOR OF THIS CHURCH AND PARISH FOR MANY YEARS. IN 1921 HE INCREASED AND RE-INVESTED THE SUNDAY SCHOOL PRIZE FUND.

CHARLES ROBERT HALL Esq OF BIDDULPH MOOR, WAS A GENEROUS SUPPORTER OF THIS CHURCH DURING HIS LIFETIME. IN 1943 HE BEQUEATHED £50 FOR UPKEEP OF THE ORGAN IN THIS CHURCH.

RECTORS OF BIDDULPH MOOR

REV. FRANCIS CORDON, M.A.	1863-1884	REV. JOHN McGUIRE, R.N.R.	1971-2000
REV. D. HIGHAM SPARLING, B.A.	1884-1902	REV. PETER TOON, M.A., D. PHIL.	2001-2005
REV. HUBERT B. BLACKMORE, M.A.	1902-1905	REV. J. ANDREW DAWSWELL	2005-2011
REV. EDWIN WHEELDON,	1905-1920	REV. DARREN A. FRASER	2012-
REV. FREDERICK N. FLETCHER, LTH	1920-1947		
REV. HAROLD WITHINGTON,	1947-1951		
REV. AUGUSTUS GOODE.	1951-1955		
REV. W. SYDNEY WILCOX.	1955-1958		
REV. W. GERAINT L. JAMES	1958-1965		
REV. IAN G. STEPHENSON.	1965-1969		
REV. JOHN MANKEY.	1969-1971		

The names of past rectors and vicars are carved in this church tablet.

10. THE FIRST YEARS

The people who filed through the doors in the decade following the opening of the church lived a very different life to the villagers of today. Almost all had been born and bred on the moor, as had their parents and grandparents before them. They'd married into other local families, were baptised amid familiar faces and faces that would remain familiar through their lives. The names written in the baptism register would be the same as those carved in the gritstone memorials in the churchyard.

Church was a gateway to the ineffable, and a passport to the hereafter for those who kept their cup level. They would dress in their Sunday Best, remember the words of the liturgy and could recite passages from the Book of Common Prayer by heart. Popular hymns were emblazoned on their memories and sung with full throats and good heart. The service was solemn, sermons long and delivered from the pulpit in uncompromising language.

Pews and benches were equally uncompromising but just wide enough to invite lethargy. This was as true for the few crinolined and sober-suited who occupied the paid pews as for their less finely attired peers opposite. Few in the congregation were robust and well-padded in the modern sense. Heights were smaller, frames more spare.

They took a hard life for granted, whether it be on their backs digging coal, tending muck-splattered sturks in midwinter, tolerating bronchial wheezes from stone dust, or the deaths of their infant children. The weather could be as unforgiving as the sermon or the pew, and they'd learnt the value of a multi-layered wardrobe early.

Hats were expected, the men removing their caps as they entered the church, the women seated in the prized bonnets they'd bought during a rare excursion to Congleton or the Potteries. They all took a pecking order for granted. The Revd Francis Gordon could read and write. He'd been Bateman's right-hand man and was on first name terms with the local who's who. He lived in an imposing rectory, by far the biggest house in the village, with its stable and carriage house. He was a pillar of the community and not to be trifled with. He was that rare thing, middle class, almost part of the gentry and a far cry from those eking out a living on their wheelbarrow farms.

Church and school were already beginning to have an impact on untutored lives. Literacy and a copper-plate hand was on the up, hymns were practised, poems learnt by heart. The church opposite was light and airy, with heated pipes to drive out the cold, a polished altar rail for communion and a pleasing ornamentation that fell between the ecclesiastical bling of High Church and the spartan interiors of the local chapels. And in the contest for souls, the orthodox church and the dissenters were running a tight race.

For in that great Victorian bid for civilization and morality, the Wesleyans and Primitive Methodists were edging ahead, particularly in poor communities where a vibrant but plainly-articulated theology with rousing hymns captured the hearts of the working classes and was delivered by them. Chapels were springing up throughout the century and particularly between 1850 and 1875, when the population was growing at an astronomical rate.

At least three substantial Wesleyan chapels - two in Bradley Green, built in 1856 and 1860, and one in Biddulph Park, built in 1860, offered Bible-inspired education and the soaring cadences of a well-attended Sabbath. All predated Christ Church, which provided an added incentive for Bateman to establish the middle ground. That's apart from a plethora of smaller, quickly-built chapels scattered across the moor.

Spellbinding oratory that hit the solar plexus and stayed throughout the week and for weeks to come sprang from the Methodist movement. But though it was a serious rival to the more sombre Church of England services, the gentry at prayer chose the wealthy orthodox church, which underpinned both monarch and state. To Bateman and his friend Hugh Henshall Williamson, whose initials HHW were liberally sprinkled on anything he owned in the vicinity of his Greenway Bank home, Methodists, Quakers, Unitarians, and the rest, were bolt-on parts. Part of the action, but lacking historic clout.

Their views were not universally shared. It all depended which gang you wanted to join, for the mid-Victorian church in England was one of schism and dissent which lingered into the 20th century and whose echoes can be felt, albeit fainter, now. As Bateman saw it, Christ Church was the true church writ in stone and stained glass. Other denominations were, if not a threat, something of which to be wary. Particularly dangerous in his view was the potential power of the Catholic Church, and he was one of many powerful Anglicans who'd objected to the funding of a Catholic Seminary in Maynooth, Ireland, out of the English purse.

It's hard for those now living in a more secular age to comprehend the depth of feeling aroused by such divisions. The children shuffling along their benches at Christ Church had their counterparts in the Primitive Chapel at Under-the-Hill and the Wesleyan Chapel at Beckfield's. There were few doubters. All were nurtured by the same creed and most believed themselves redeemed in making the journey to church or chapel once, sometimes twice on a Sunday. Making their way along unmade lanes and field paths, the common coin was survival in an unforgiving world, and if God provided a helping hand, that was all to the good no matter how you worshipped.

The church on the moor imparted solace to the sick and newly bereaved, the imprint of the cross fashioned in holy water from the lead-lined font to the new-born and ceremonial joy to the betrothed. And the course of unremembered lives was painstakingly recorded by the Revd Francis Gordon in the marbled registers purchased in Burghope's in Congleton for a guinea a time.

Baptisms

In the decade from 1863, 118 boys and 114 girls were baptised by Francis Gordon, an average of one a fortnight. (By comparison, in 2012 there were three baptisms throughout the year.) Even this large number doesn't tell the whole story: there were more births than baptisms, and some parents would have opted for their children to be baptised elsewhere.

Bearing in mind the population of the 'district' was around 1200, the number

Compare the two church interiors.

The first picture shows the church as
it was before 1903, when a new pulpit
and hymn board were installed.
Oil lights can also be seen.

The second picture, below, was taken
after 1937, when electric lighting was
made available for the first time.

seeking baptism was substantial and outnumbered the 135 burials which took place at the same time by almost two to one. In Biddulph Moor, as in the rest of Britain, families were large and the population was undergoing a steep upward climb despite high rates of mortality.

The age at which infants were baptised varied. It was not uncommon for older children and young adults to be baptised, or for family groups of children to be baptised together as religious observance grew in strength. However, the common preference, then as now, was between one and three months after birth. Life was precarious; baptism was a blessing conferred upon those who may not live to maturity. In the decade following the church's consecration, the font was rarely out of use.

Four generations at Christ Church. Retired farmer Jim Nixon holds his great grandson, while his son and grandson look on.

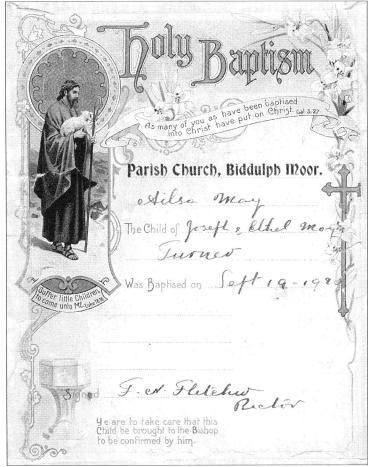

Ailsa Booth née Turner's certificate of baptism was signed by Revd Fletcher (1920-47) on September 19th, 1920.

Burials

Neither was the graveyard, particularly where infants were concerned. Anyone with a passing acquaintance of life expectancy during the Industrial Revolution will already be familiar with the scourge of infant mortality. Few Victorian novelists failed to create at least one character who died an early death or had a narrow escape from its clutches.

Fiction writers tweak reality, and reality in the 19th century was as bad, if not worse, than that depicted in their stories. The situation on Biddulph Moor was no different from the rest of the country, indeed, slightly better than that in the urban slums thrown up by industrialisation.

But 'slightly better' still meant that in that first decade children of five and under accounted for almost 55% of all burials which took place at Christ Church. Of these, 9% died within a week of their birth, almost 7% between a week and a month old, a huge 20% between a month and a year old and almost the same percentage up to the age of 5. In contrast, the number buried after their 70th birthday was only 7.5% of the total - in the first ten years, only eight parishioners survived into their 70s and two their 80s out of a total of 135 burials.

The statistics make chilling reading. The good news is the dramatic improvements made over the next decades, not least due to better health care as introduced through such movements as Hospital Saturday, the National Health Service and improved nutrition. Predictably, the Burial register of the time records peaks in February and March, when the struggle to keep warm was at its height and winter was drawing to a close.

Poignant statistics, echoed throughout England and heart-rending for the modern reader, are the multiple bereavements suffered by some moorland families. Burials of several siblings and adults living in the same house are not uncommon over the ten year period; the burial lists record one instance where the ages of the deceased range from 4 months, 2 years, 9 years, 19 years, 44 years to 78 years old. Of these, four died within two years of each other, including a young mother and her child.

Britain might have then been the richest country in the world, but life was precarious for all, and death a constant visitor. The certainty of an afterlife was essential if hope was to survive.

Marriages

Though in one instance the groom was 18 and his bride 16, a typical age for groom and bride was 25 and 23 respectively. Three quarters of all brides married an older man, and in 15% of marriages the groom was younger. Almost all marriages were between local partners; those few from further afield

The Revd Fletcher was rector from 1920 to 1947.

lived in Leek, Horton, Lask Edge or Bradley Green.

The witnesses to the wedding were usually relations of the bride or groom. Occasionally a husband and wife together would bear witness to the marriage. If a witness wasn't available, Elizabeth Gordon, wife of the minister, would stand in.

Sixty-two marriages took place between 1864-74, about one every two months. Some fathers gave away more than one daughter, and it wasn't unusual for the fathers of both bride and groom to know each other through working in the same place.

The Revd Hubert Blackmoor, rector for three years until his early death in 1905. His daughter Dorothy, beside him in the trap, visited her father's church in 1967.

Names

All three registers are a primary source of local surnames, and an indicator of the changing fashion in first names. Marriage entries are particularly useful, since the Christian names of two generations appear on the same certificate and these can point to changes in the rank of popular names in the intervening years.

Bearing in mind the three registers typically cover an age span of six decades, the most frequently

Biddulph Moor, July, 1905.

To the grief of the whole Parish, we have this month to record the death of our late beloved Rector, the Rev H. B. Blackmore, who ; though he had been with us only for three short years, won the hearts of his Parishioners as few men could have done.

His happy and cheery disposition, coupled with his great desire for his Master's Glory, and his earnest longing to win souls for Him whom He knew to be his own Saviour, gained for him the affection of all with whom he came in contact.   One of his favourite hymns was No 30 in Hymns of Consecration and Faith, in which occurs, -

" Work on, then, Lord, till on my soul
Eternal light shall break,
And, in Thy likeness perfected,
I " satisfied " shall wake."

He is now in the presence of the Saviour, realizing what in these words he longed to be his experience.   Truly God's ways are unsearchable but we bow to His decision, knowing that He makes no mistakes; and pray that His richest blessing and consolation may rest upon his sorrowing widow and relatives, to whom we tender our sincerest sympathy.

Hubert Blackmoor, whose ministry lasted three years before his early death in 1905, is commemorated in the Parish Magazine.

used first names of the 1820s were James, John, William, Thomas and Samuel. By the 1840s the order had changed slightly to William, Thomas, John, Joseph and George;

BIDDULPH MOOR:

August, 1903.

My Dear Friends

You will all be pleased to hear that we are to have, in the early autumn, a BEAUTIFUL NEW PULPIT erected in our church. It is a gift which we shall all greatly prize, because it will be in memory of her whose removal from our midst has been such a terrible loss, not only to this parish, but to all who knew her; also because of the giver, Mr John Cole, whom we all esteem so greatly, and lastly, because it will greatly enhance the appearance of our Church. There is yet another gift which is to be made very shortly for the adornment and use of our church in the shape of a handsome OAK HYMN-BOARD, by our kind and generous friends Mr and Mrs Myott. We are more grateful than we can possibly say to them and also to our various friends who have been so liberal to us in helping us to make the necessary improvements. We have been much encouraged by their kind interest and sympathy, and trust that others will be moved with the same spirit.

Hubert B Blackmore.

ANNUAL REPORT ON THE SCHOOLS.

MIXED SCHOOL

" The School continues to be well taught and disciplined "

INFANT SCHOOL

" The School is in good order and the teaching has been successful. "

Marriages	May 6th, Ernest Stonier and Sarah J Sutton.
	„ 27th Richard Hulme and Minnie Shufflebotham
	July 12th, Ernest Mayer and Mary A Cottrell,

Funerals.	May 7th,	Timeson Lancaster,	aged 39 years.
	„ 16th,	John Bailey,	„ 50 „
	„ 21st,	Annie Cottrell	„ 25 „
	„ 26th,	Mary Cole	„ 43 „
	June 30th	Harriet A Brooks,	„ 10 days.
	July 12th,	James Gibson	„ 2 „

Baptisms.

May 10th,	Maria, ...	daught of	Joshua and	Hannah Lovatt.
June 14th,	Edith Mary, „	„	George „	Hannah Doorbar.
„ „	Gladys Matilda „	„	Albert „	Jessie Corbishley
„ „	Lilian Beatrice „	„	Henry „	Elizabeth Beech.
„ 19th,	John, ...	... son of	Benjamin &	Hannah Edge.
„ 27th,	Harriet Ann, daught of		Paul and	Edna Brooks.
July 12th,	Lizzie. ...	„	Jonathan „	Ellen Cottrell.
„ 9	James, ...	son of	Nathan „	Elizabeth Gibson.
„ 12	William Harold „	„	Thomas „	Elizabeth Plant.
„ „	Bertie,	„ „	Walter „	Mary J Gee.
„ „	Alfred,	„ „	Henry „	Elizabeth Machin.

BM Parish Magazine, Aug 1903, records Revd Hubert Blackmoor's pleasure at the gift of a new pulpit and hymn board.

and by the 1860s, William, Joseph, John and Thomas. This narrow pool of first names was common to all regions of the country, and is echoed in the choice of female names. The 1840s gives us Sarah, then Hannah, with Elizabeth/Ann, Mary/Harriett and Jane/Martha sharing 3rd, 4th and 5th place. By the 1860s the position had shifted to Hannah, Elizabeth, Mary, Sarah Ann and Harriett.

The adventurous names now taken for granted didn't exist in mid Victorian Britain. The range was limited, and even over four decades few additions were made. There were, however, some exceptions. During the 1860s/70s middle names became fashionable, and combinations of Thomas Charles, John Thomas and Joshua Edward for boys and Mary Ann, Mary Ellen, Sarah Ann and Sarah Jane for girls became prevalent for the first time - along with such Biblically-inspired boys' names as Abraham, Job, Isaac and Cephas. On very rare occasions a girl's parents would buck the trend altogether and opt for a more exotic Tabitha or Melinda, with Emerson making a rare male appearance.

Surnames weren't subject to the vagaries of fashion, and the local names common at the end of the 18th century showed no sign of flagging by the middle of the 19th. In the burial registers, by far the most frequently listed name is Bailey, followed by Brown, Beech, Plant, Stanway, Simcock, Nixon and Hulme. In the Marriage Register - mainly couples born in the 1840s - Bailey again heads the list, followed by Brown, Shufflebotham, Stanway, Sutton, Pass, Smith, Cotterill and Wood.

In common with sparsely-populated villages and towns throughout the country, this narrow band of surnames could lead to confusion. Hence the practice, adopted elsewhere, of allotting a distinguishing nickname: the Baileys, for example, could be Blueys, Flattens, Pinkies, Slappers, Timothies, Tidleys or Watlers. None of these found its way into the church archive.

Occupations

Biddulph Valley was rich in coal, and many small pits were scattered along its length. In 1860, Robert Heath and the railway arrived and within a few years Black Bull was employing more than all the minor pits together.

It will come as no surprise, therefore, that almost 50% of all Biddulph Moor grooms in the decade 1864-74 gave their occupation as collier. (By the early 20th century the word 'collier' had been superseded by 'miner'.) Next in frequency was 'labourer', which accounted for 29% of the occupational total. Two other jobs had a strong showing: farmers (11% of total) and masons, at 5%.

By comparison, out of a total of 62, 23 fathers of brides and grooms termed themselves labourers, 7 masons and only 5 colliers. These men were born a generation earlier and seemed to have stuck with their original work despite the overwhelming increase in coal production. It was their offspring who saw the way the wind was blowing. The labourers produced 7 sons who were colliers, the farmers 7 and the masons, 3.

Other occupations among those Biddulph Moor fathers born around the 1820s were: smith, shoemaker, earthenware dealer, publican, butcher, tailor, potseller, weaver, coal-seller, packer, cattle-dealer, and grocer. The last seven of these all had

Bible Study Group 1950. Revd Withington in centre.

collier sons. A generation later, hawker, salt-seller, gardener, miller and domestic servant would be added to the list. Women's occupations, if any, were not widely given in church registers until the 1940s, though censuses from the 1860s do record these.

Close to home
Leaving the moor a hundred and fifty years ago was no easy task. All but one of the names recorded in the burial register at this time lived within a stone's throw of the church, and many of the places they hailed from are familiar today, such as The Hollands, Smithy, Naylor Bank, Hot Lane, Slang and Crowborough. Marriage partners were almost exclusively from the immediate vicinity, the few exceptions being from neighbouring districts such as Horton, Lask Edge, Bradley Green and, in one instance, Leek.

Signatures and crosses
In his poem Forefathers, Edmund Blunden captures rural life not only in his childhood Kent, but in much of England before widespread schooling was introduced. Lines from one verse in particular could describe any one of a thousand villages which remained largely untouched by the thrust to industrialise.

'Scarce could read or hold a quill,
Built the barn, the forge, the mill.'

These lines are especially poignant, for illiteracy was high throughout the country but practical accomplishments, often passed from father to son, were essential in communities which couldn't readily rely on outside help.

Biddulph Moor was no different. The school opened in 1852, and couples taking their vows at Christ Church in the 1860s/70s had been born too early to benefit from a formal education. The generations before were even more disenfranchised.

Of the 62 marriages which took place between 1864-74, 55% of all bridegrooms couldn't write their own name. Their brides suffered an even greater disadvantage, with an illiteracy rate of 65%. This latter statistic was reflected throughout much of the country and explanations are varied: there was no imperative for women to learn since most had no outside occupation to encourage it; there was also a reluctance by some

of those in authority to give girls an opportunity to 'rise above their station' - one of the indicators of 'station' being the acquisition of literacy skills. In addition, there is anecdotal evidence to suggest that in some cases literate women would deferentially 'make their mark' alongside that of their husband.

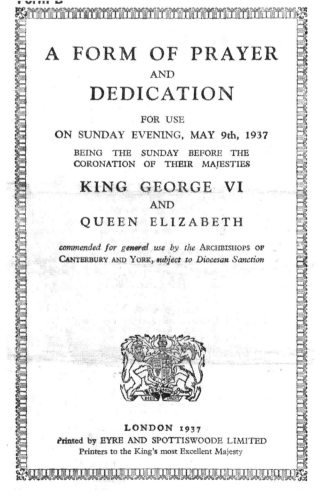

Half the marriages were between partners signing only 'his mark' and 'her mark' and a cross. Only in around a fifth of entries were both bride and groom able to read and write.

There is some evidence that male literacy was dependent on occupation. Samples suggest that farmers and masons, where costing, estimation, and signed receipts were important to their trade, were 100% and 66% literate respectively, compared to the 40% of colliers who could read and write and 20% of labourers.

But changes were afoot.

Revd Fletcher's special service to mark the coronation of King George V1 and Queen Elizabeth, shortly after the abdication of the King's brother, Edward.

11. CHURCH AND MOOR: CHANGES AFTER 1873

Literacy

The author's great grandfather was an illiterate collier at the time of his wedding. Yet his son, the author's grandfather, was an avid reader of the *Evening Sentinel* and could be found in his chair behind the football scores into old age. His generation had been schooled; his father's hadn't.

The National School at Biddulph Moor not only taught the 3Rs; it introduced scholars to good behaviour and the Ten Commandments; to folk-songs, elementary arithmetic and rhyme. It taught letters chalked on slate, later blot-free copper-plate verse in ink recited in class and committed to memory.

And the results were impressive. Each decade from the 1870s delivered a massive improvement in literacy. An overall average of only 41% of all those marrying in that first decade were literate. By the 1880s the figure had risen to 68%, and by the 1890s 79%. By 1904, 95% of all brides and grooms could sign their names in a clear hand, and by the end of the Great War this had reached the 100% mark, where it remained.

Miriam Leese is a gifted local organist who continued to play at Christ Church during many of the evening services after she left the area. In the mid 60s, when this photo was taken, the organ was sited within the transept. It was later re-sited under the transept arch.

Incomers

Other changes were afoot. As transport developed and roads improved, Biddulph Moor became less isolated and work in neighbouring towns became possible. In the first ten years of the church's life, only 1 out of 12 bridegrooms were from outside the village, and they lived locally. By 1900, this proportion had risen to 1 in 9, with addresses as far away as Reddish, Mossley, Congleton and Salford. In the years up to the Great War this proportion increased to almost 1 in 5, with Mow Cop, Chell, Bosley and Rushton among the addresses given.

The cessation of hostilities produced an even greater influx of bridegrooms from Macclesfield, Newchapel, Gratton, Rushton, Endon, Cheadle, Bemmersley, Leek, and Stockport. Now 1 in 3 had been born and brought up outside the area. By the 1930s, almost half of all bridegroom originated elsewhere, and in addition to an increase from such neighbouring towns and villages as Leek and Macclesfield, far-flung Loughborough and Cardiff claim a mention.

By the 1950s, almost 72% of bridegrooms were from outside the village. Some remained in the village after marriage; others took their new brides back to their home towns or set up home in an area new to both. Whichever course was chosen, one inescapable conclusion is that over the decades women had gradually joined the workforce, and a regular bus service meant that employment in nearby towns, where they met their partners, beckoned.

Plummeting mortality rates

Just as dramatic was the steep decrease in mortality rates for children of five and under. In the 1860s/70s this group formed 55% of all recorded burials at Christ Church. From then on it fell decade by decade. The percentages tell their own story: 48% (1880s), 43% (1890s), 33% (1900s) 30% (1910s), 15% (1920s), 12% (1930s), 4% (1940s). The decrease in average family size throughout the period contributed to these statistics, yet the underlying trend remains valid.

These improvements were paralleled by an equally impressive rise in the age of the deceased. In the first years, little more than 7% of those entered in the Burial Register had reached 70 or more. This fraction rose almost year on year throughout the 19th and 20th centuries, becoming 9% (1880), 13% (1890), 12% (1900s), 14% (1910s), 19% (1920s), 33% (1930s, 1940s), and over 51% (1950s).

Only the early years of the 20th century bucked this trend, and neither the flu epidemic following the Great War nor the war itself appear to have curbed the rise in life expectancy.

New Names

Favourite Christian names continued to follow the dictates of fashion, and although John, William, Thomas and James remained popular choices for boys into the 1950s, their ranking varied and other first names gained in popularity - particularly Sam and Richard in the 1880s, Fred and Herbert in the 1920s, Edgar, Jack, Richard and Harry in the 1940s and Arthur in the 1950s.

The time-honoured staples of Mary, Martha, Hannah, Jane, Sarah and Elizabeth also underwent tweaks and changes for the girls. By the 1940s/50s, the variety of choice was wide enough to knock the decade-by-decade 'Mary' from its pole position. 'Hannah' fell behind in the ratings for the first time in the 1930s, and the popularity of 'Jane' had been eclipsed by the 1890s. New appearances included 'Emma' (1890s), Charlotte and Eliza (1900s), Florence/Flossie (1920s), Laura and Beatrix (1930s) and Winifred (1940s).

More jobs

The prominence of the main four occupations, given in the early records - collier, farmer, labourer and mason - fluctuated over the next eighty years, but the general trend for two of them - labourer and mason - was downwards. Masons in particular

Parishioner Hannah Shufflebotham presented two communion cups to the church on her 80th birthday to replace those given by Francis Gordon in 1863. The choir is flanked by Terry Williams (left) and Revd McGuire (right) Photo 1990.

didn't figure in the records after around 1920, when better transport links and industrial processes made building in brick competitive.

Those describing themselves as farmers also showed a downward trend between 1900 and the 1930s, though the years of World War Two and after showed a sharp increase due to the government's efforts to increase domestic food output.

The position of mining is especially interesting. Colliers formed 46% of the Biddulph Moor workforce in the 1860s. As the population grew and industries, enabled by the railways, expanded, this percentage rose sharply. By the 1870s, the proportion of Biddulph Moor workers describing themselves as colliers had leapt to 63% of total male employment, and this had only dropped to 58% as late as the 1920s. Black Bull and Whitfield collieries absorbed much of the manpower. By the 1930s, although tonnage increased, mining was beginning to benefit from mechanisation and to shed labour. A wider range of jobs was also becoming widely available. Now miners accounted for less than 45% of the workforce.

This was still considerable, but a far-cry from its peak at the end of the 19th century, when a coalmaster such as Robert Heath was responsible for the welfare of entire streets of miners' families. During the 1940s, further developments in mechanisation, spurred by the demands of war and aided by conscription, reduced the numbers working in the pits to a mere 15% of total. This fell to 14% in the first years of nationalisation, where the widespread use of machinery secured an even greater tonnage produced by a fraction of the workforce.

Throughout the first fifty years of the 20th century, a small percentage of the workforce gave 'bricklayer' as their occupation. This had peaked at 11% in the 1890s, when Bradley Green was growing rapidly and the population here and elsewhere needed houses. Soldiers on leave also make a showing (19% of total) in the Second World War. By the 1930s, employment was far wider in scope than could have been conceived by those living in the village during the first years of the church. Male occupation had broadened to include clerk, plasterer, grocer, lorry driver, mechanic, postman, sheet metal worker, baker, joiner, haulage contractor and boiler maker.

The upsurge of building after World War Two also gave rise to joiners, painters, bricklayers and fitters. Engineering, in meeting the demands of returned peace, needed mechanics and welders, while transport drivers, bus drivers and conductors, lorry drivers and both mechanical and electrical engineers were necessary to service much-improved transport links.

From the mid 1940s onwards, women's labour was recorded for the first time in the church archive. Occupations as varied as canteen worker, clerk, weaver, teacher, kitchen maid, typist and machinist provide ample evidence of a mobile female workforce making daily journeys from the moor to the nearby towns.

Bateman, Gordon, Cooke and Stanway

James Bateman left Biddulph Grange to his son John in 1870 - who sold it to Robert Heath - and moved to a house he'd rented from Edward Cooke in London's Hyde Park Gate South. He served as a magistrate in the city for some years before moving to Worthing on the south coast. Here he began a new, more modest garden, but still found time to marry his wife's maid, Annie Goss, after the death of Maria. He died in 1897, the year after Biddulph Grange was rebuilt by Robert Heath following a disastrous fire.

The Revd Francis Gordon's ministry lasted until his death at the Rectory at the age of 72 in July, 1884. His wife, Elizabeth, had passed away two years earlier at the age of 60. He was succeeded by the Revd Higham Sparling, who continued as rector until 1902. After his ministry, Sparling returned to Lancashire, where he was born. He died in 1916 at the age of 76.

Francis Gordon and his wife are buried in separate graves behind the chancel. The third rector of Christ Church, Hubert Blackmore, who died at the end of a three-year ministry aged only 38, is buried nearby. He was survived by his wife, Jenny, who he married at Kendal in 1895, and his nine year old daughter, Dorothy (who paid a last visit to Christ Church in 1967). At the time of writing, 15 rectors (latterly, vicars) have served the church.

Edward Cooke, who sketched the original ideas for a 'church for the moor' kept in touch with members of the Bateman family after Bateman left the Grange, especially Bateman's son, Robert, who, like Cooke, was an artist, and who kept a studio in Biddulph Old Hall. Robert was also a frequent visitor to *Glen Andred*, Cooke's home in Groombridge. Cooke died there in 1880, aged 69.

Francis Gordon's grave,
situated behind the apse.

**Christ Church has
changed little since
it was built in 1863.**

Builder Joseph Stanway and his wife, Harriett, were born in Biddulph around 1820. After their marriage in 1841 they moved to Biddulph Moor. His eldest sons, Joseph, John and William were, like Joe, stonemasons. In 1861 his younger children Edward, Peter, Richard and Robert were scholars at Biddulph Moor National School. His 17 year old daughter, Ellen, was a silk piecer - a mender of broken threads. The 1881 census shows Joe, Harriett and their son, Robert, now 24, living in a cottage on Biddulph Moor. Joe and Robert are both shown as stonemasons. Harriett died in 1886, aged 66, leaving Joe a widower.

By 1891 Joe, now aged 72, was living with his son Robert and Robert's wife, also Harriett, in New Street. Three years earlier, Joe was recorded as a trustee of the newly-opened New Road Church: at some point he had become a Wesleyan. The date of his death is inconclusive, but he doesn't appear on the 1901 census. By then his son

This 1903 Parish Magazine points to an active programme of worship.

The glass and aluminium screen erected in 1978 by Revd John McGuire.

Robert, and Robert's wife Harriett, had moved to a different New Street address and Robert was employed as an underground hewer. Robert died in 1921, aged 65, and his wife in 1916, aged 61. They are buried together in the old Christ Church graveyard.

Developments on the Moor

What was Hot Lane rectory - formerly parsonage - looks much as it did when it was built in 1863. A new rectory was built in its grounds, later a tennis court, in 1979. The older building was sold to a private purchaser in the same year. The new rectory was similarly sold in 2006. Currently, vicars live in Park Lane, Knypersley, and their ministry now extends to both St John's and Christ Church.

Francis Gordon was recorded in the 1861 census as living in Moor Parsonage, Hurst. At the time there were only two properties down Hurst Bank, of which his was one. When he vacated the house in 1863, it was sold or rented to local families and referred to as the Old Parsonage in marriage and burial records. This name seems to have died out around 1870, possibly owing to confusion with the address of the 1863 parsonage. Among those giving Old Parsonage as their address are Levi and Mary Cottrell (1868). Three years later they had moved to Church Cottage at the end of Church Lane.

Biddulph Moor churchyard was extended towards Woodhouse Lane in 1975 to provide additional burial space. A Garden of Remembrance was added in 1979, and a Lych Gate five years later. Much of the Glebe land between the two schools was sold to private developers in the early 1980s, leaving only a small parcel behind the old school, leased by the PCC.

The original roadside classrooms which formed the National School in 1852 remain, along with the school house once occupied by the head teacher. As the school population rose, more room was needed. To meet the demand, the hall was added in 1885 - provided by the new owner of the Grange, Robert Heath.

When the council school was built in 1908, the older children transferred there, leaving behind the infants' section. The infants occupied the old school until 1942, when they, too, moved to the council school, leaving the original school to the Ministry of Defence. At the end of the war it became Christ Church Hall, the present Parish Room reflecting its original use as a place of worship. The schoolhouse was enlarged and modernised in 1904.

The church itself has undergone minor changes. A new pulpit was erected in 1903. The boarded floor, which had begun to rot, was replaced by a solid concrete and parquet floor in 1979; the font had been moved from the back of the church to the front six years before.

An attractive glass and aluminium screen was built in 1978 during Revd John McGuire's ministry as a buttress against draughts from the main doors. The pipe organ, which had become too expensive to maintain despite a generous bequest of £50 by Mr Charles Hall in 1943, was removed in 2011, thereby enabling the future conversion of the transept into a useful community space and integrating it once more into the body of the church.

The memorial window dedicated to Francis Gordon and installed by Higham

Revd Gordon's successor, Higham Sparling,
had this window made in Gordon's memory.

Sparling a year after Gordon's death was refurbished in 2004, thanks to money raised by and a generous donation from Mrs Gwen Lancaster. A memorial window to the well-loved Hubert Blackmoor was also installed in 1906. The oil lamps which had lit the building for more than seventy years were finally taken down when electric lights replaced them in 1937. Piped water arrived in the mid 1930s.

A new Primitive Methodist church to replace the chapel at Under the Hill was built in Chapel Lane in 1904, although it would be a further six years before the chapel shed the last of its congregations. New Road Church was built in 1887 and opened a year later, using stone carted from the dismantled Beckfield's Wesleyan chapel by William and Joseph Lancaster in part of its construction. Both the Chapel Lane and New Road churches were more substantial buildings than the chapels they replaced; the Wesleyan church also encouraged the Methodist commitments to education by building a Sunday School in 1886 which was later integrated into the main building.

The lanes to Biddulph Moor were tarmaced in the 1920s in readiness for regular bus services and to facilitate the growth of the private car. The 1960s saw a vast expansion of the village, as mass housing made its first appearance and the population mushroomed. Commuting to work in the Potteries or one of the neighbouring towns became a fact of life for the author and many others. The congregation of Christ Church rose in consequence of this influx.

Despite the march of history, the church remains a focal point in the village. Perched unthreateningly on its modest hill, its distinctive rose window keeps an eye open for friends and strangers alike.

A future historian might wish to look into its further evolution. 2063 will mark its bicentenary. Maybe that will be a good time to do it.

Bill Ridgway, 2013

The Church

A group of us went to the church. We went around the outside I noticed a lot of Baileys on the grave stones. The church is a round shape it is like a cross. We went inside the building of the church in some glass it was a book of remember remember all the people that had died. (We) In the church there was a bell we all had a go of it. On the floor there was a picture of a dove it was a nice picture. I put a choir frock on and a hat. We went out side again and had a look at a Litchgate.

Successive rectors have maintained close links with the local school(s).
One enthusiastic youngster recalls his visit to the church.

Enoch Yeomans makes short work of the churchyard grass in this 1950s shot

Herbert Reeve, church organist and head of Biddulph Moor School, played a full part in village life life and is buried in the churchyard.

A family group line up to celebrate the baptism of Hannah Porter, held by mother Kay centre. Kay's husband Rob and Hannah's sister Jessica, right, Kay's sister Donna, extreme left. Other family members: Jean Alcock, Ann Mellor, Jane Alice Mellor and Joan Porter.

The Breakfast Club in the Church Hall has been a popular venue in recent years

Church members, family and friends enjoy a lively Christmas in 2009,
with entertainment by a local jazz group.

Members of the churchyard team in 2009.
L-R: Bill Ridgway, Ann Walker, Kevin Dunn, Jack Bodsworth

Getting the church spruced up for another year.
Alf Pound, by the glass door, casts a professional eye over the new paintwork.

Dan and David Stoker take lessons from cake-maker Evelyn Bodsworth as their mother Ruth looks on. Harry Marsh in the background contemplates a treat.

Nita Nicholls sells another plant at the Church Plant Sale, an annual event in the Church Hall.

Getting ready for refreshments. The Church Hall kitchen comes into its own at this pre-Christmas get-together. Ann Gadsden and Hilary Williams at counter.

Christ Church and what became the new churchyard looking less manicured in this early photograph.

The Holiday club in the Church Yard in 1978.
L-R Adults standing: Revd John McGuire, Terry Williams, Margaret McGuire, lay-reader Bill Bailey, Dorothy Scragg stooping, front row, left.

A church carriage.
Fiona Bailey holds the reins in the Church Hall yard, while horseman Bill Bailey walks behind, 1978. Shortly after the oil tank and coal store were removed and the brick yard tarmaced.